TWO PROCESS PHILOSOPHERS

AAR STUDIES IN RELIGION
Number Five

TWO PROCESS PHILOSOPHERS

Hartshorne's Encounter with Whitehead

by
WILLIAM LAD SESSIONS
Washington and Lee University

DAVID R. GRIFFIN
Claremont School of Theology

WILLIAM M. O'MEARA
Madison College

FREDERIC F. FOST
Linfield College

CHARLES HARTSHORNE
University of Texas

LEWIS S. FORD, *Editor*
Pennsylvania State University

Tallahassee, Florida
American Academy of Religion
1973

Library of Congress Catalog Card Number: 73-85592
ISBN Number: 0-88420-104-X

Copyright © American Academy of Religion

PRINTED IN THE UNITED STATES OF AMERICA
PRINTING DEPARTMENT, UNIVERSITY OF MONTANA, MISSOULA, MONTANA 59801

Contents

CHAPTER I

Hartshorne's Encounter with Whitehead: Introductory Remarks

Lewis S. Ford

For many today, process theology primarily means the joint impact of Whitehead and Hartshorne. Some, under the tutelage of William A. Christian at Yale, have taken their Whitehead straight; others have explored his more empirical aspects under the guidance of Bernard Loomer or Bernard Meland or Daniel Day Williams. Most, however, while admiring the subtleties and wide-ranging inquiries of Whitehead into mathematics, physics, biology, sociology, epistemology, and the history of philosophy, have found in Hartshorne a reliable guide both for an independent understanding of process theism and for the interpretation of Whitehead's philosophical theology. Hartshorne's clarity of presentation and argument, coupled with a freedom from Whitehead's neologisms, has made him a most influential exponent of process thought, and many read their Whitehead through Hartshorne's spectacles.

This was certainly true in my own case. As a Yale undergraduate I heard a good deal about Whitehead from a roommate, whose enthusiasm for his philosophical hero was infectious. I was put off, though, by esoteric vocabulary he needed to explain Whitehead to me. I knew *Adventures of Ideas* was being taught in one of the introductory courses, and I had worked through A. A. Bowman's sympathetic critique of the early Whitehead[1] in a course with Charles Hendel. But all of this had made very little impact on me. Then one Friday afternoon when I was leaving for a weekend date at Mount Holyoke, my roommate handed me a copy of Hartshorne's *The Divine Relativity* to read in a spare moment. That night after a delightful evening I picked up the book for a bit of bed-time reading, and read until four in the morning. I often get engrossed in novels or general nonfiction and find them hard to put down, but that rarely happens with serious works of philosophy and theology. This book was the exception, and I finished it before the weekend was over. I found the argument utterly convincing, and was instantly converted to process theism, though for many years I hoped it was subsumable under the Tillichian framework I espoused in those days. The next day, working in the *Review of Metaphysics* office in Linsley-Chittendon Hall, I unexpectedly learned that Hartshorne was passing through New

---

[1] A. A. Bowman, *A Sacramental Universe*, ed. J.W. Scott (Princeton: Princeton University Press, 1939).

Haven that very day, and managed to wangle an hour's excited conversation with the master that afternoon—interrupting, I fear in retrospect, his customary afternoon nap. That summer I began *Process and Reality*—so sleepy after working ten hours in the fields that I would have to stand to read—finding it both very intriguing and most baffling. Thereafter for years Whitehead and Hartshorne became so entwined in my own thinking that I could never be sure where one left off and the other began.

For those sharing this predicament, David Griffin's essay on "Hartshorne's Differences from Whitehead" is most timely. The similarities between the two thinkers are so broad and overwhelming that their differences have been neglected, but these are very real and must be taken into account for an adequate appreciation of the intricate interrelationship between them. Griffin has worked through the Hartshornian corpus with an eye toward culling all the differences Hartshorne notes between his own philosophical position and Whitehead's. He proposes seven basic differences: (1) God is a single actual entity for Whitehead, but an unending temporal series of divine occasions for Hartshorne, each fully including its predecessors; (2) Hartshorne denies any need for the eternal objects, seeing specific possibilities as temporally emergent; (3) Hartshorne takes secondary qualities (such as colors) to be first emergent in the experience of high-grade sentient organisms, while Whitehead argues that the same sensa are ingredient in the low-grade occasions prehended (e.g. molecules) as in the prehending high-grade occasions (of e.g., human experience), though functioning in diverse ways; (4) Hartshorne's philosophic method and concept of metaphysical principles is more uncompromisingly rationalistic than Whitehead's (though Griffin finds this contrast has been largely overdrawn, more apparent than real); (5) Hartshorne once held that contemporary occasions could prehend one another, but now agrees with Whitehead they cannot; (6) Hartshorne denies that the subjective immediacy of occasion is lost in being taken up into God's consequent experience, while it is a disputed point of interpretation whether Whitehead thought otherwise; and (7) Hartshorne denies any real genetic succession within a single actual occasion, finding Whitehead's talk of "earlier" and "later" phases to be misleading. Of these, the first two are the most important and the most widely known, though their implications have rarely been fully explored. The third difference is perhaps least known, and Griffin has done yeoman's service in making it available to us.

Griffin's essay is also timely for another reason, for Hartshorne's essays on Whitehead have recently been republished in a single volume: *Whitehead's Philosophy: Selected Essays, 1935-1970.*[2] This is a superb introduction to Whitehead's thought by the one independent thinker whose metaphysical vision is most closely attuned to his. Of course, as Hartshorne himself makes plain, his "primary aim has always been to arrive at truth

2 Lincoln: University of Nebraska Press, 1972. 217 pages. $7.95 (hereafter, WP).

through Whitehead, or to make truth accessible to others through him, more than to ascertain or communicate the truth about Whitehead" (WP 3). Thus the book is not so much a commentary on Whitehead's text as an independently reasoned defense of a broad range of characteristic Whiteheadian theses—those which Hartshorne finds most basic, most insightful, and most sound. It does not introduce us to Whitehead's works or specialized vocabulary,[3] nor are the intricacies of his mature system spelled out in detail, but we are most forcefully introduced to his *ideas*. Because most of the essays do not presuppose a prior acquaintance with Whitehead on the reader's part, it can be safely recommended to those seeking a painless but reliable avenue of access to Whitehead's metaphysics, particularly his philosophical theology. Save for a brief introduction, all of the essays have been previously published, though not all have been equally accessible.[4] Hartshorne has added some brief bracketed passages reflecting his present thinking on his earlier essays,[5] but these carry no new surprises: Hartshorne's interpretation of Whitehead remains fairly constant over the years, and the few shifts have been carefully noted (WP 3).

Two Process Philosophers, while functioning also as an independent inquiry into Hartshorne's relationship to Whitehead, may be conceived as a companion volume commemorating the publication of *Whitehead's Philosophy*. Though Hartshorne has briefly noted his differences from Whitehead (WP 2), his essays perforce dwell on the dominant similarities. Here Griffin's essay can serve as an appropriate corrective, as well as an extended critical review from one particular vantage point. It, like the other essays in this volume, was substantially completed before the appearance of *Whitehead's Philosophy*, but we have cross-listed all references to its pages. While Griffin makes use of additional writings for his analysis,[6] the presence of these particular essays in one book, essays which have been scattered throughout various journals and anthologies over the past thirty-five years, considerably facilitates the comparison of these two thinkers.

This comparison requires us to probe deeper than the acknowledged differences. Accordingly, in "Whitehead's Differences from Hartshorne" I have tried to view the problem from a Whiteheadian perspective, and propose four additional differences: (1) the laws of nature are divinely imposed

---

[3] Though see chapter 12, "Whitehead and Ordinary Language," defending several of Whitehead's neologisms and special uses of words.

[4] The asterisked items in the bibliography, section two, list its contents according to their original sources.

[5] The most extensive addition may be found on p. 27; see also, e.g., pp. 103, 113, 118, 206, 206f. The inclusion of three words, "or just after," on p. 103 nicely illustrates Hartshorne's lively awareness that he no longer holds that God can prehend contemporary occasions.

[6] Particularly Hartshorne's other books, but also further articles: see Griffin's footnotes. Save for some important reviews and replies, *Whitehead's Philosophy* contains Hartshorne's published writings on Whitehead in the main. One important exception should be noted: "Religious Bearings of Whitehead's Philosophy," chapter 14 in *Reality As Social Process* (Glencoe: Free Press, 1953 and New York: Hafner, 1971).

for Hartshorne, while they are immanent for Whitehead, expressing the regularities of causal inheritance; (2) lacking a doctrine of eternal objects, Hartshorne cannot explain divine persuasion in terms of providing initial subjective aims, (3) nor can subjectivity be understood in terms of subjective aim; finally, (4) their concepts of "panpsychism" differ. More importantly, the issue over the eternal objects appears differently from a Whiteheadian perspective. Through Hartshorne (and Paul Weiss) I have come to appreciate Peirce's insistence upon the continuity of possibility and its temporal emergence, which in Hartshorne's eyes conflicts with the apparent discreteness and permanence of the eternal objects. So it would, if God in every successive moment must prehend all of the eternal objects distinctly, as he must on the divine society model. But Whitehead's God is a *nontemporal* actual entity, who nontemporally prehends the eternal objects, prehending them temporally only part of the time. Whitehead permits nontemporal as well as temporal actuality and this, I argue, is at the root of the most of their differences. Many Whiteheadians, unknowingly perhaps, share Hartshorne's restriction of actuality to temporal actuality, and therefore have been persuaded that God must be reconceived as an unending series of occasions. If so, they ought to follow Hartshorne's lead in renouncing the eternal objects, but few have been induced to do so. For my own part, I find Hartshorne's critique against permanent, discrete eternal objects fully persuasive, but not applicable to Whitehead, whose eternal objects can be conceived as continuous and as temporally emergent (insofar as they are relevant to temporal actualities).

Except for my own, all the essays for this monograph were written independently of one another. Nonetheless they are closely related. Those by William M. O'Meara and Frederic F. Fost pick up and develop the fourth and fifth differences, respectively, which Griffin has catalogued. O'Meara defends Hartshorne's conception of metaphysics as the study of non-restrictive, existential affirmations, seeing it to be a valid extension and clarification of Whitehead's methodology. Fost focusses upon Hartshorne's initial disagreement, and subsequent agreement with Whitehead that contemporaneous occasions cannot prehend one another. In his dissertation,[7] Fost shows the intimate connection between the mutual prehension of contemporaries and Hartshorne's idealistic understanding of the world's inclusion within God, an understanding ultimately deriving from Josiah Royce. Here Fost explores the ramifications of Hartshorne's subsequent agreement with Whitehead, arguing that it has generated some unresolved or partially resolved tensions in the formulation of his philosophical theology.

Any comparison of these two process thinkers must finally ask: is Hartshorne a Whiteheadian? The question is ambiguous. Obviously he is if by this we mean that the affinities sufficiently outweigh their differences so as

    [7] "The Philosophical Theology of Charles Hartshorne: an analysis and critique of the categories of dipolar theism." Diss. Claremont, 1964. 301 pp.

to permit their common classification. The more significant aspect of the question concerns how we account for these affinities. Is Hartshorne basically Whitehead's disciple, developing his own arguments to defend his master's theses? Or is he primarily an independent thinker, encountering Whitehead only after having firmly established the basic contours of his own thinking? Are the striking similarities a fortunate accident, or are they genetically derived? Content for many years to stress the common theses he shares with Whitehead, Hartshorne has more recently stressed his independent concerns, most notably, his defense of the ontological argument.[8] Perhaps the best way to answer these questions would be to study Hartshorne's writings prior to his encounter with Whitehead in September 1925. This is the task William Lad Sessions has undertaken in his examination of Hartshorne's unpublished Harvard dissertation of May 1923, "An Outline and Defense of the Argument for the Unity of Being in the Absolute or Divine Good."

Sessions shows that nearly all of the characteristic theses of Hartshorne's mature philosophy are present in the dissertation, and hence he is not Whitehead's disciple. Nonetheless he persuaded me that Hartshorne is more of a Whiteheadian than I have been inclined to suppose in recent years. Somewhere Hartshorne has described his early philosophy as a synthesis of James and Royce, with an assist from William Ernest Hocking. I therefore imagined it to be primarily a synthesis of James's pluralism with Royce's monism, viewing God as dependent upon the world for the ever-increasing plurality he includes within himself. Then the only important novel element Hartshorne would have learned from Whitehead would be the theory of unit-occasions of becoming, a theory which could easily be incorporated into this prior philosophical strucure. Thus I was not prepared for the basic monism of the dissertation, which remains a monism even if qualified by the admission of contingency and of some external relations.[9] One senses that Hartshorne was struggling to affirm more freedom, more open-endedness, more creativity than his monistic conceptual framework will permit. What was primarily needed was a conceptual device for reconciling monism and pluralism, and this Hartshorne seems to have found in Whitehead's concept of prehension, correctly interpreted as an asymmetri-

[8] In "The Development of My Philosophy," pp. 211-18 in *Contemporary American Philosophy: Second Series*, ed. John E. Smith (London: George Allen & Unwin, 1970), Hartshorne divides his intellectual career into four periods. "The third period began abruptly in September, 1925, when I became a humble member of the Harvard philosophy staff, and was asked at one and the same time to begin editing the writings of C. S. Peirce and to assist Whitehead in grading papers" (p. 217). During this period, "from 1928 to, say, 1945, it was plausible to think of me as Peirce's and even more as Whitehead's disciple" (p. 218). "The change to what I term my fourth period, one of greater independence, or greater stress upon my own intellectual devices and spiritual convictions, was gradual. The sharpest shift probably occurred in 1958 while I was in Japan" (p. 219) and began to think through the centrality of the ontological argument with a new thoroughness.

[9] *Ibid.*, p. 214.

cal relation, internally related to the prehender but externally related to that which is being prehended.

The early Hartshorne also needs a viable doctrine of God's two natures. Sessions remarks that "Hartshorne does say many things in the dissertation which in a later context would be ascribed to God's concrete consequent nature" but he "had not fully, or not clearly, broken away from the traditional conception of an *actus purus* or monopolar God." Now exactly the same thing can be said of Whitehead's Lowell Lectures of February 1926, published in *Religion in the Making*. Its God is essentially the God of Plato and Aristotle, capable of being conceived impersonally as the Form of the Good embracing all other forms within itself or personally as the Unmoved Mover, inspiring all other beings but itself affected by none, contemplating only its own thoughts, a sheer concrescence of pure conceptual feeling. Somehow, in the space of two years, Whitehead thought his way through to an understanding of God as also being affected by and enriched by the world, something the dominant tradition of Western philosophical theism has been unable to achieve in two thousand years. His prior analysis of an actual occasion as possessing both physical and conceptual prehensions clearly contributed to this novel conclusion, once the anomalous character of God as having merely conceptual prehensions became apparent.

First, however, in order to recognize that his concept of God was an anomaly, Whitehead would have to agree that God must exemplify the same metaphysical principles as other actualities. In *Science and the Modern World*, God is simply the *principle* of limitation, a very abstract principle variously called "Jehovah, Allah, Brahma, Father in Heaven, Order of Heaven, First Cause, Supreme Being, Chance" according to different systems of thought.[10] By the time of *Religion in the Making*, this principle of limitation has been reconceived as an "actual but non-temporal entity," but it is not yet an actual entity among other actual entities as in *Process and Reality*. For it can be conceived either impersonally as a principle, or personally as an actuality, and it is grouped not with actual occasions but with creativity and eternal objects as the "formative elements" which jointly constitute the character of the actual occasions. Then in his Harvard lectures for 1926-27 Whitehead enunciated six main principles of his metaphysics, adding that "the principles apply to all actualities, including God."[12] One of these principles is called the Ontological Principle, defined by the thesis that "the character of Creativity is derived from its own creatures, and expressed by its own creatures." This is the obverse of the Spinozistic monism Whitehead espoused in *Science and the Modern World*, but it it not yet the "principle of efficient, and final, causation" the ontological principle comes to be in *Process and Reality* (pp. 36f). If, however, White-

---

[10] *Science and the Modern World*, p. 257.

[11] *Religion in the Making*, p. 88.

[12] Victor Lowe, "Whitehead's Gifford Lectures," *The Southern Journal of Philosophy* 7/4 (Winter, 1969-70), 332f.

head was inclined to interpret even this early Ontological Principle as entailing the general Aristotelian principle that there is ultimately only one species of actualities, this may have induced him to avoid making God an exception to his metaphysical principles. Another of these six early principles, the Principle of Solidarity, stipulated that "every actual entity requires all other entities in order to exist." If so, God would have to be internally related to all the actual occasions, and this would require divine physical prehensions. Thus to the nontemporal actuality of pure conceptual feelings of *Religion in the Making* there must be added a second, consequent nature of physical feeling.

Did Hartshorne derive his dipolar theism from this line of reasoning? Some of his remarks suggest otherwise, for he lists "the two-aspect view of God (which I got from Hocking if from anyone) as both eternal and yet in process" as a belief which he had already adopted, but which Whitehead deepened and encouraged.[13] This has been clarified somewhat in private correspondence. Hartshorne writes: "All I got from Hocking about God was simply the conviction that the future must be open, partly indeterminate, even for God—thus really open. It is stretching things to say that this is already a two natures view of God. But if, as Hocking and I did, one takes for granted that God has certain perfections (e.g. perfect knowledge) primordially and everlastingly, and yet acquires new determinations as "the indeterminate future becomes the determinate past" (Peirce, note), there must be an immutable as well as a mutable aspect of divinity." So there must, *unless* we espouse some kind of concrete universal, as Hartshorne apparently did in his dissertation. For if the ultimate universal is supremely concrete, the "mutable" particulars might be somehow conceived to be included within and taken up into the "immutable" universal. At least Hartshorne in 1923 has no firm doctrine that the universal is always abstract, while the concrete is always particular, which would necessitate a dipolar conception of God if God has both universal features and acquires new determinations.

In the dissertation God is the inclusive whole, but God and the creatures jointly determine what is, transforming an open future. He is a personal being involved with his creatures. The logic of Hartshorne's basic convictions generates a pressure in favor of dipolar theism, but the monistic doctrine of the concrete universal holds him back. What is most needed is a way of distinguishing and uniting the concrete and the universal. This Whitehead's theory of prehension could provide, analyzed in terms of asymmetrical internal relatedness. Then the universal is abstract, externally related to the concrete, while the concrete is particular, partially constituted by the ab-

---

[13] "The Development of My Philosophy," p. 216f. See also two related comments: Whitehead "posits a divine Becoming rather than mere Being—an idea which duplicated a conviction I had acquired from Hocking's metaphysics class about 1921" (p. 223). "Hocking did convince me in a very brief discussion, but once for all, that my perhaps only momentary toying with the idea of an immobile deity, devoid of an open future, was a mistake" (p. 224).

stract. In the case of God, his abstract universal essence is included within his changing, particular temporal states. This line of reasoning may have been achieved concurrently with, and even independently from, Whitehead's discovery of the consequent nature, but the doctrine of prehension appears to be a necessary link.

It is important to recognize that the theory of two divine natures resolves different problems for our two process thinkers. Whitehead's God already enjoyed the entire wealth of conceptual possibility, but he was only very thinly personal, being wholly cerebral, absent-mindedly aloof from worldly affairs. The problem was to render him more personal, more involved in the world, and this was effected by adding physical feelings to his conceptual feelings and integrating the two. Hartshorne's God was already personal and all-inclusive. Dipolarity permitted a clear distinction between the universal and the concrete, such that the divine essence could be conceived as included within (prehended by) God's concrete states.

If this difference is overlooked, it becomes all too easy to conceive Whitehead's primordial nature along Hartshornian lines as a permanent atemporal abstract essence always included within the everlasting consequent nature. This permanent essence is somewhat complicated by the fact that it includes all specific possibilities as well, while Hartshorne has streamlined it down to those necessary properties God must at all times exemplify. If one wonders how God can unify his experience, which could then only be in terms of the consequent nature, one is tempted to postulate with Hartshorne an unending series of temporal divine unifications. But the primordial nature is not an inert, abstract essence; it is a conceptual activity, a concrescence of conceptual feeling—a thinking on thinking, if you will. It is an abstraction from the total reality of God, deficient in actuality, and devoid of consciousness, but this does not render it simply abstract in the sense of being an eternal object or a multiplicity of eternal objects. It is a unity of conceptual feeling, devoid of consciousness insofar as it is unintegrated with physical feeling. The consequent nature does not include the primordial nature in the sense in which a prehending occasion includes some datum prehended, for we are here considering the way in which various prehensions are integrated together. Whitehead's language may be misleading, for he refers to the consequent nature ambiguously as the totality of divine physical feeling and as its integration with divine conceptual feeling. Once it becomes possible to see the primordial nature as a concrescence of feeling rather than as a realm of eternal objects, it may become possible to conceive God's unity in such a way that it makes eminently good sense to speak of God, as Whitehead characteristically does, as *the* nontemporal actual entity. This becomes obscured, however, if we allow the issues which led Hartshorne to affirm divine dipolarity to dominate our understanding of Whitehead's God.

But I should not be allowed to have the final word on this. Thus we are fortunate to have Hartshorne's own brief listing of the characteristic theses of process philosophy, with succinct judgments of the special contributions Peirce, Whitehead, and he himself have made to this enterprise.

In the bibliography I have listed all the books and articles by our two process philosophers that are cited in the essays. The list of books is arranged alphabetically according to the abbreviations used, for the convenience of readers who may become puzzled by some of the symbols given in the citations.

CHAPTER II

Hartshorne's Early Philosophy

WILLIAM LAD SESSIONS

Charles Hartshorne's philosophy is frequently viewed as essentially derivative from Whitehead and, to a lesser extent, Peirce. Typically, Hartshorne has been called the most notable of Whitehead's "intellectual descendants."[1] The purpose of this paper is to show the mistakenness of such a view, primarily by closely examining Hartshorne's unpublished doctoral dissertation, written before he had made significant contact with either Peirce or Whitehead.[2] Whether or not Hartshorne and Whitehead share the "same" philosophy in any systematic sense, this sharing cannot be explained historically, since Hartshorne simply did not *derive* most (nor perhaps the most basic) of his philosophical tenets from Whitehead. Historically or biographically speaking, therefore, Hartshorne is not a "Whiteheadian." The potential importance of this fact must not be underestimated. Once it is seen that Hartshorne does not derive his philosophy from Whitehead, it becomes possible, indeed imperative, to reconsider whether Hartshorne's doctrines mean the same as Whitehead's, even when they are couched in similar (or even identical) language. Recognition that Hartshorne is not, in the main, an intellectual stepchild of Whitehead therefore *may* allow us, in our more systematic moments, to view "dipolar panentheism" or "neoclassical philosophy" on its own terms and in its own right.[3]

In the process of showing the nature and extent of Hartshorne's independence from Whitehead, three further themes will emerge:

(1) Most, though not all, of Hartshorne's mature positions and lifelong

---

[1] Delwin Brown, Ralph James, and Gene Reeves, eds., *Process Philosophy and Christian Thought* (Indianapolis: Bobbs-Merrill, 1971), p. v.

[2] This paper will focus on Hartshorne's relations to Whitehead, even though similar claims could be made concerning his relations to Peirce.

[3] By no means do I wish to deny either the obvious agreements and similarities between Hartshorne and Whitehead, nor the patent fact that Hartshorne has long been an influential and sympathetic interpreter of Whitehead. But I *do* wish to deny that either fact warrants calling Hartshorne a "Whiteheadian" in any strong sense. Mere agreement, if not historically derived, would also allow us with equal right to call Whitehead a "Hartshornean"; and interpretation, even sympathetic interpretation, of a thinker implies at best mere agreement and not derivation. Further, I do not mean to imply that what unites Hartshorne and Whitehead is less important or true than what divides them. Nevertheless, recent criticism, in my opinion, has over-stressed the unity at the expense of the diversity, thereby leading to a distorted view of Hartshorne's own contribution. If I perhaps distort in the direction of diversity, it is in hopes of helping to correct the prevailing and opposite distortion.

concerns in philosophy, though not the later technical language and arguments, are to be found in his dissertation, submitted at the age of twenty-five. Hartshorne's intellectual career has consisted chiefly of a gradual ramification of certain broad-gauge views and interests solidly established early in his life. One might view his career as the search for language suitable to express his early—almost adolescent—insights. On this view, claiming that Hartshorne is a "Whiteheadian" simply amounts to saying that Hartshorne has seen Whitehead's language as more suitable than most for expressing such insights as he had already gained.

(2) Most, though not all, of Hartshorne's initial and sustaining insights derive from, or at least are most intelligible in the context of, not "process philosophy" (whatever such a term might mean prior to Whitehead), but Nineteenth-Century Idealism. Idealism provides not only the form, language and a good deal of the polemical ammunition but also many of the central tenets of Hartshorne's dissertation, and it is illuminating to view his later writings from the same perspective.

(3) Most, though not all, of Hartshorne's later writings, which in purpose and content are inexplicable if viewed as stemming from the stimulus of Whitehead, are illuminated by the concerns of his dissertation. For example, Hartshorne's continued interest in the psychology of sensation, the ontological argument, philosophical theology and the nature of metaphysics are all deeply rooted in his dissertation. Hartshorne is not a Whiteheadian disciple who has chanced to explore areas of experience which were left largely uncharted by the master. Rather, his apportionment of time and energy is dictated more basically by his own characteristic themes and purposes.

I.

Before examining Hartshorne's dissertation, it is useful to glance at his intellectual career,[4] which may be divided into four periods. The first peri-

---

[4] Here I rely chiefly on what Hartshorne has said in "The Development of My Philosophy," pp. 211-28 in *Contemporary American Philosophy, Second Series,* ed. John E. Smith (London: Allen and Unwin, 1970). See also the prefaces to *The Philosophy and Psychology of Sensation* (hereafter, PPS), *Reality as Social Process* (hereafter, RSP), and *Creative Synthesis and Philosophic Method* (hereafter, CSPM), as well as the following essays: "Whitehead and Contemporary Philosophy," pp. 21-43 in *The Relevance of Whitehead,* ed. Ivor Leclerc (London: Allen and Unwin, 1961), reprinted in *Whitehead's Philosophy: Selected Essays, 1935-1970* (hereafter, WP), pp. 141-60; "On Some Criticisms of Whitehead's Philosophy," *Philosophical Review* 44 (July, 1935), 323-44 (WP 21-39); "The Monistic Theory of Expression," *Journal of Philosophy* 50 (July 2, 1953), 425-34; "Causal Necessities: An Alternative to Hume," *Philosophical Review* 63 (October, 1954), 479-99; "The Social Structure of Experience," *Philosophy* 36 (April and July, 1961), 97-111; "Tillich and the Other Great Tradition," *Anglican Theological Review* 43 (July, 1961), 245-59; and "Idealism and Our Experience of Nature," pp. 70-80 in *Philosophy, Religion and the Coming World Civilization,* ed. Leroy S. Rouner (Hague: Nijhoff, 1966). See also Hartshorne's remarks in *Philosophical Interrogations,* ed. Sydney and Beatrice Rome (New York: Holt, Rinehart and Winston, 1964), pp. 319-54.

od (1912-19) covers the years before entering Harvard as a junior. Philosophical influences during these years, as recalled by Hartshorne, were chiefly Rufus Jones, Royce, James, Augustine, Emerson, Matthew Arnold, Coleridge, H. G. Wells and Amiel. "In spite of the limited philosophical fare, I reached (about 1918) some metaphysical convictions which I still see [in 1970] as sound—in part for the reasons which I then had in mind. The convictions reduce in a way to two."[5] First, experience has "an essentially social structure" in that all experience consists of the direct apprehension of the feelings or experiences of other sentient beings. Hence it is not an inference but a matter of direct experience for Hartshorne both that there are other sentient beings and that sentience is not confined to people or even to animals. Our experiences of all other beings are really our experiences of *their* experiences. This view Hartshorne claims to have reached "on phenomenological grounds," i.e., as a matter of direct insight and not from books.[6] Second, experience has a "monistic aspect" in that the many sentient beings are somehow united or "included" in one supreme being. Once again this view had a "partly phenomenological basis" in the experience of value as requiring an "all-inclusive aim" which is satisfied only in an "inclusive self."[7]

Hartshorne's second period (1919-1925) covers his four years at Harvard and two years of postdoctoral study in Germany. During this period he wrote his dissertation, as he says, "uninfluenced by Peirce, and only slightly influenced by Whitehead, of whom I knew only what a hasty skimming of *The Concept of Nature* and an enthusiastic report by Northrop of his studies with Whitehead in London could teach me."[8]

The third period (September 1925-ca. 1945) encompasses years of editing the Peirce papers, assisting in one of Whitehead's courses, and then expounding the thought of both men—years of "intensive influence from two great minds."[9] During this time, Hartshorne remarks, he considered himself "as both a 'Peircean' and a 'Whiteheadian,' in each case with reservations." Peirce's influence appears to Hartshorne to have been less than Whitehead's "chiefly because his writings are on the whole less congenial to the philosophical attitude I already had when I encountered the work of the two thinkers."[10] It is important to stress this point. *Both* Peirce's and

---

[5] "The Development of My Philosophy," p. 211.

[6] *Ibid.*

[7] *Ibid.*, pp. 212f.

[8] *Ibid.*, p. 214. See below for Hartshorne's actual, as opposed to his remembered, use of Whitehead in his dissertation.

[9] *Ibid.*, p. 215.

[10] *Ibid.*, p. 216. Hartshorne goes on to say that he learned Whitehead's philosophy "chiefly from his books," although this seems to conflict with an early article in which he asserts that "my first acquaintance with most of his (Whitehead's) ideas was by means of the spoken rather than the written word." See "On Some Criticisms of Whitehead's Philosophy," p. 323 (WP 21). Settlement of this point makes little difference, since whether by spoken or written word Hartshorne cannot have learned of Whitehead's mature philosophy in any detail before 1925,

Whitehead's influence consisted in the revision and reinforcement of a previously adopted position, and not in the introduction of anything fundamentally new. According to Hartshorne, "A good part of the effect of Peirce and Whitehead was to encourage beliefs already adopted."[11] A partial list of these antecedent beliefs would include the following:[12]

(1) Metaphysics or "*a priori* ontology" and natural theology must be sharply distinguished from "empirical cosmology" as regards its aim, methods and content (a distinction which Hartshorne believes "both Peirce and Whitehead tend to blur").[13]

(2) Experience has a social structure; other concrete realities are immediately given in experience.

(3) Experience has a qualified monistic aspect; all entities are somehow "included" in one entity yet they are not totally determined by that entity. (Hartshorne indicates William James recalled him from an early though brief fling with determinism.)

(4) Experience is ultimately valuational and aesthetic in nature.

(5) There can be no mere "matter"; reality consists of "feelings"; hence psychical categories are primary and some form of idealism is true.

(6) Both internal and external relations are real.

(7) There are two aspects to God (a view which Hartshorne says he got from W. E. Hocking's metaphysics class "about 1921," although he does not seem to utilize it in his dissertation).

Of course, not all of Hartshorne's beliefs antedate his contact with Peirce and Whitehead; he did learn something new from both men. What is perhaps surprising, however, is how little he acquired from them when compared with what he already believed.[14] Hartshorne learned from Whitehead that:

(A) The final or ultimate realities are actualities or event-atoms (here Hartshorne does regard himself as indeed a "disciple" of Whitehead).

(B) Both memory and perception are temporally structured; prehension is the basic form of dependence or ontological relation.

the publication date of *Science and the Modern World* as well as the beginning of Hartshorne's assistantship to Whitehead.

[11] *Ibid.,* pp. 216f.

[12] See *ibid.,* pp. 211-19, RSP 18f, "Causal Necessities: An Alternative to Hume," p. 490n6, and "Whitehead and Contemporary Philosophy," p. 21 (WP 141f).

[13] "The Development of My Philosophy," p. 219.

[14] Cf. Hartshorne's remark that "It was so long ago that I can barely recall how it was, but I may have learned more metaphysically from Emerson's Essays (illogical as they are) and Wordsworth's and Shelley's metaphysical poetry (from which Whitehead also profited) than by reading and hearing Whitehead" (CSPM xvii).

(C) Contemporary events are mutually independent (although Hartshorne only came to this view "when I was no longer very young and he [Whitehead] was no longer alive").[15]

(D) "Personal immortality" is "beside the point," and only Whitehead's "objective immortality" solves "the problem of the transitoriness of life."[16]

(E) Whitehead's technical language is superior in precision to Hartshorne's previous (mostly Idealistic) language.

In the last several decades Hartshorne claims to have moved gradually into a fourth period, "one of greater independence, or greater stress upon my own intellectual devices and spiritual convictions."[17] During this time, his voluminous writings have been concerned mostly with the ontological and other arguments for God's existence, the nature of metaphysics and its relation to philosophical theology, the vitality and validity of Idealism, and the social structure of experience. The stress upon these topics is best construed not as Hartshorne's breaking free from Whitehead's intellectual shackles, but rather as a return to topics characteristic of his earliest writings and lying at the heart of his own independent philosophical approach.

Our discussion of Hartshorne's earliest philosophy (before 1925) will take the following course: Section II outlines the main structure and themes of Hartshorne's dissertation, Section III considers the mentioned sources of this work, while Sections IV-VI focus on some of its more important doctrines and positions: IV on the method of metaphysics and its relation to natural theology, V on a few important metaphysical doctrines, and VI on the doctrine of God.

II.

Hartshorne's dissertation, approved by the Harvard Department of Philosophy and Psychology in May, 1923,[18] bears the impressive title of "An Outline and Defense of the Argument for the Unity of Being in the Absolute or Divine Good." Though cumbersome, the title does manage to summarize the dissertation's basic thrust. Hartshorne is concerned to argue for what he calls "teleological monism" (= "the Unity of Being in the Absolute or Divine Good"), a doctrine which consists of two parts (OD ld):[19] (a) "There is one ultimate or uncompounded Principle or Reality, such that all things must be conceived as necessarily contained or present

[15] "The Development of My Philosophy," p. 224.
[16] "Whitehead and Contemporary Philosophy," pp. 21f (WP 142).
[17] "The Development of My Philosophy," p. 219.
[18] Hartshorne's readers were William Ernest Hocking, Henry M. Sheffer and Raphael Demos.
[19] OD designates the dissertation by its short title, "An Outline and Defense." OD page numbers followed by "d" refer to the seven-page digest.

within its unitary nature or life" (Monism). (b) This all-inclusive Reality is the supreme instance of value, where value is "essentially a matter of social relations" and hence, in Hartshorne's view, inseparable from experience. The One Reality "contains" all things by experiencing or valuing their experiences or values. Hence "the relation of the Many to the One becomes that of the valued to the valuer. Interest or appreciation, in a *Perfect* form, must register within its own life of significance all the qualities of its objects —so far at least as these are of value" (Teleological Monism). The "One Reality" is both a universal principle in its scope and a concrete individual in its "life of significance."

"*The* argument" for Teleological Monism is really a structured *series* of arguments concerning various basic (or metaphysical) "root-ideas or categories" (OD 86). The categories considered are Being, Individuality, Quality, Relation, Space and Time, Knowledge, Value, and Perfection. They are ordered in terms of the advance from abstract to concrete, so that each successive category renders "more explicit" the Ultimate One or Monistic Principle and hence interprets and resumes all of the other categories (OD 82f, 88). Concerning each category, Hartshorne argues that pluralistic and absolutistic accounts are equally inconsistent and inadequate, thereby leading inexorably upon reflection to the admission of the truth of Teleological Monism. Consideration of each category is therefore "a phase of the necessity for a Monistic view of Being" (OD 82). Either all things are ultimately one in the comprehensive or inclusive life of the supreme, perfect or "Divine" being, or else, Hartshorne believes, the latter notion is absurd, in which case

all life and thought, with its criterion or ideal of perfect or wholly true knowledge and perfect or completely socialized and beneficient personality, is oriented inalienably toward self-contradiction and all consciousness implies the inconsistency of the self-existent Perfect as without that self-reality which is of its very essence. (OD 7d)

The ultimate goal therefore is not merely to prove the abstract (or perhaps "non-existential") truth of Teleological Monism, but also to make this truth a self-possession, to unite all "powers of the mind," as Hartshorne puts it, "in a single ultimate attitude, affirmation, or consciousness of truth" (OD 85).

III.

Anyone who instinctively associates Hartshorne with Whitehead will soon be struck in reading this dissertation by the notable near-absence of any favorable reference to "process" thinkers (with the possible exceptions of Bergson and Varisco) in footnotes or bibliography. Peirce is not mentioned at all, and Whitehead's name appears only twice, once in a short, out-of-context quotation from the *Concept of Nature* at the outset[20] and

[20] Hartshorne quotes only Whitehead's sentence, "The values of nature are perhaps the key to the metaphysical synthesis of nature." But Whitehead follows this sentence with: "But such a synthesis is exactly what I am not attempting." *The Concept of Nature*, p. 5.

again in Hartshorne's chapter on Space and Time, where several passages from Whitehead's "fascinating book on 'The Principles of Natural Knowledge'" are quoted in support of Hartshorne's contention that magnitude is relative to an absolute and non-quantitative standard (OD 173-77). "The most impressive realistic metaphysician of today" (OD 24) is not Whitehead but Alexander.

The names Hartshorne does mention are chiefly his contemporaries, especially Idealists and their critics. Outside of Plato ("the great founder of Teleological Monism" [OD 15]), Spinoza (condemned for denying freedom), Kant (whose doctrine of experience as essentially non-valuational is "on the whole a monstrous fabrication" [OD 213]) and Hegel (whose concrete universal is identified with Plato's Idea of the Good, and both with Hartshorne's Monistic Principle), references to the philosophical tradition are infrequent.[21] Instead, Royce, Bradley, Green, MacTaggart, J. Ward, Gentile, Bosanquet, N. O. Lossky, J. S. MacKenzie, J. E. Creighton, Hartmann, even Swedenborg (OD 255) and Walter Pater (OD 198)—all enter the lists at one point or another on Hartshorne's side; while Russell, R. B. Perry, E. G. Spaulding (who is probably mentioned more frequently than anyone in the dissertation), F. C. S. Schiller and William James are his favorite sparring partners. Of course, mere mention does not prove dependence, nor does omission indicate independence. Still, the evidence does suggest that *whatever* the sources of Hartshorne's early thought, Whitehead and Peirce probably were not among them, and they were at least congenial to Idealism. At any rate, whether or not Hartshorne did derive his early philosophical convictions from Idealists, he at least quickly saw his enormous kinship with Idealism and utilized its language, arguments, structure and method in his dissertation.

IV.

In Part I of the dissertation, which consumes slightly less than one-third of the text, Hartshorne advances the following picture of the nature, aims and method of metaphysics (or simply "philosophy," as he usually calls it): Philosophy is "a rational inquiry into the meaning of life as a whole" (OD 60) and hence of one's own life; it is

> a last stand of the reason, a final return of knowledge from the region of possible error to the assured certainty which it enjoys in the possession of itself, as the self-verifying source and ground of all inquiry. (OD 61)

Any philosophical assumptions, particularly methodological ones, must conform to such a characterization of philosophy. One such assumption is that philosophical knowledge (and indeed any knowledge at all) involves some kind of experiential intuition:

[21] Nevertheless, Hartshorne still maintains that the "meaning" of the history of philosophy is a deepened perception of the meaning and truth of Teleological Monism (OD 91).

to know *is not merely to believe or to infer from premises.* It is at bottom to *see,* to possess, to hold inalienably within oneself. . . . To know you must have or possess experientially, in the end. (OD 62, 142)

Not only knowledge but truth itself is a matter of experience: "For us truth is not at the last a matter of propositions but of possession, enjoyment, or harmony" (OD 169). Since for Hartshorne the "harmony" of experience is the agreement, coherence or consistency of the intentional contents of experience, it follows that for him consistency is the test of truth and inconsistency of falsity:

the basis of philosophy is an insight belonging to mind into the success of its own combinations of meaning to serve its own fundamental or unitary purpose: into, in other words, the consistency of its ideas. (OD 63)

Not only cannot the inconsistent be thought, it cannot even *be,* since being and consistency are "known somehow" "in an identity" or as self-evidently coextensive (OD 64). Since all knowledge and truth are matters finally of experience, and experience is valuational for Hartshorne, it follows that all knowledge or "ideation" is valuational. Only idealism is able to account for this "working principle" of philosophy (OD 67).

The concepts or "ideas" of philosophy, Hartshorne insists, are communicable (or "transferable," to use his term which points to the experiential basis of conception), but only partially so, because (1) obscurity is directly proportional to concreteness, and good philosophy plunges thought into the concrete; and (2) if the universe is "spiritual," philosophical truth *may* be veiled by defects of character; one *may* have to be a good man to be a good philosopher (OD 69-71). Hartshorne therefore is willing to admit that he may be understood only by other Idealists or even only by himself (OD 69), because, he says, he prefers imperfect communication to bad philosophy (OD 72). Still, communicability is at least a proximate goal, and Hartshorne roundly condemns the philosophical doctrine of "indefinabilism," as regards both concepts and doctrines: As regards concepts, Hartshorne holds that there are no wholly indefinable or isolable ideas, but rather "all concepts are the expression of a common principle or life" which is grasped more or less (mostly less) fully (OD 73). There is thus a certain circularity to philosophical inter-definition, but it is not a vicious circularity, since each term has its own prior, though partial and inadequate meaning (OD 78). Still, "the *full* meanings of all words depend on a full consciousness of their relations, as forming the system in which, as functions of the One Mind, they are organized" (OD 74n1). There is also a "scale of ascending concreteness among concepts" (OD 74) at the same time that these concepts are "interpenetrating ideas, not an aggregate of distinct entities but modes of viewing substantially the same object or feature of reality" (OD 97). As regards doctrines and principles, metaphysical assertions and arguments form an interconnected system. Thus Hartshorne speaks of his arguments as "cumulative" re-expressions of the same basic content, where each successive "phase" or chapter incorporates everything preceding as "a more abstract or relatively blind expression of the same truth" (OD 88).

Philosophy in Hartshorne's earliest view is therefore the more or less communicable expression of a directly experienced systematic view of reality—or rather it is the *endeavor* to accomplish this, since there can be no dogmatic finality in philosophy (OD 302). At the very least, one cannot know that everything relevant has been considered, or that all possible objections have been overcome.

> Metaphysics, thus, . . . is but a fair suggestion or hint, when tested by its own ideal. It is but a word of reasonable advice, weighty but not wholly imperious or commanding, which is offered to the reflective man. (OD 303)

Hartshorne does not wish to claim a complete demonstration of indubitable consistency on the grounds of the finitude of human thought (OD 59), but he still holds out for what he calls a "principle of relative truth" (OD 58), which he expresses by means of a metaphor: Philosophy is a never-ending quest or voyage, yet it sails under an "Eternal Sunshine" which indicates "the sole possible *direction of escape* from the contradictions inherent in the partial abstractions . . . of the ordinary understanding" (OD 58). There is a suggestion here, supported by the actual course of Hartshorne's philosophical career, that final philosophical *insight* can be achieved, although, in Whitehead's words, "the merest hint of dogmatic certainty as to finality of *statement* is an exhibition of folly" (PR x; emphasis added).

Concerning this understanding of philosophy, two comments are in order: First, it is remarkable how little Hartshorne's position has changed. Although he has perhaps come to an increasing sense of the difficulty of being "right" in philosophy and has considerably modified the language in which he describes philosophy, the basic emphasis on philosophy as experiential insight into the "meaning" of all reality has remained undiminished. This suggests that in Hartshorne's view the shifting vehicles and baggages of philosophy are ultimately of less importance than the enterprise itself.

Second, Hartshorne's Idealistic understanding of philosophy should be carefully distinguished from Whitehead's method of speculative philosophy. We have already noted Hartshorne's remark that Whitehead (and Peirce) tend, in his opinion, to blur the distinction between *a priori* philosophy and empirical cosmology. But further, whereas Whitehead's speculative philosophy is "the endeavour to frame a coherent, logical, necessary system of general ideas in terms of which every element of our experience can be interpreted" (PR 4), Hartshorne's method is chiefly to exhibit the necessity for a valuational monism by exposing the inconsistencies in opposing views. One might say that whereas Whitehead proposes (his own speculative scheme of categories), Hartshorne disposes (of what he takes to be contending views). As a result, Whitehead's writings are filled with interconnected *aperçus* while Hartshorne's are mostly argumentative. It is arguable that these differences—whether of emphasis or substance—

have roots in more than biography, that Hartshorne accepted Idealism's quest for the One True System in a way that Whitehead never did.

Natural theology in Hartshorne's dissertation—as, indeed, throughout his life—is all but indistinguishable from metaphysical philosophy in content, source and method. First, philosophy concludes to a One, "one Ultimate Being, one 'all-general and all-sufficient principle' or 'World-Ground'" (OD 1). But the One is also the Good, and "the Good ultimately is the Divine (OD 4). Second, while philosophy's task of accounting for the whole of things leads it to seek data from any source, still it must give priority to religious data:

> In the end philosophy must descend into the full concreteness of experience if it is to get its abstract or logical outlines filled with any significant meaning. It must rely above all upon that most profoundly empirical of all modes of apprehension—the religious. Otherwise it will fail, as in a measure philosophy has always failed, simply for lack of sufficiently profound (i.e., spiritual or valuational) conceptions to deal with. . . . a just comprehension of genuinely religious concepts supplies the sole possible basis for a consistent and all inclusive synthesis of experience. (OD 23, 37)

Third, natural theology's method is to show that and how alternative categorial systems (those denying the possibility of a One or necessary being) are inconsistent, incoherent and inadequate.

The Ontological Argument—to which a long chapter is devoted in the dissertation—is for Hartshorne a paradigm of argument in natural theology or metaphysics, with the added advantages of making explicit the full existential and conceptual claims of the conclusion. The Ontological Argument, Hartshorne says, aims at showing that if the concept of Perfection or "the Ideal Personality" or "the Perfect Mind" is "an absurdity" or inconsistent, then

> all life and thought, with its criterion or ideal of perfect or wholly true knowledge and perfect or completely socialized and beneficent personality, is oriented inalienably toward self-contradiction and all consciousness implies the inconsistency of the self-existent Perfect as without that self-reality which is of its very essence. (OD 7d)

Hartshorne's meaning is far from transparent, but perhaps it can be clarified in the following way. The general form of all of Hartshorne's metaphysical arguments seems to be this: If the metaphysical concept of X (e.g., Being, Knowledge, etc.) is inconsistent, then experience cannot be consistently conceived, and the fundamental motivation of thought will be frustrated. Now to this schema the Ontological Argument adds (or, Hartshorne would probably say, makes explicit) two features: (a) The concept of X is consistent only if the concept of a *perfect* X (e. g., perfect being, ideal knowledge, etc.) is consistent, so that the concept of a perfect X shares the necessity of the concept of X. (b) The concept of a perfect X is such that if it is consistent it follows that there *is* a perfect X; the possibility of a perfect X entails the actuality of a perfect X. In this way the Ontological Argument makes explicit Hartshorne's belief that the fundamental thrust of our consciousness towards consistency of understanding will be frustrated and our whole life fragmented unless we assent to the existence of a perfect being, for assent to an actual perfect being is required by any coherent account of experience. Thus the basic goal of metaphysics, to arrive at a consistent system of concepts by reducing opposing alternatives (which Hartshorne believes can be exhaustively specified) to "absurdity," can be satisfied only by a system in which Perfection is consistently conceivable, which is to say one in which the Ontological Argument is valid.

This view of theology and philosophy has persisted throughout Hartshorne's career. In a recent discussion, for example, Hartshorne says that a "theistic proof" "establishes a price for rejecting its conclusion, and in this way clarifies the meaning of the latter. It helps to measure the gap between belief and disbelief" (CSPM 276). Further,

> All the arguments are phases of one "global" argument, that *the properly formulated theistically religious view of life and reality is the most intelligible, self-consistent, and satisfactory one that can be conceived.* (CSPM 276)

Such a statement, which could have come directly from Hartshorne's dissertation, supplies a clue as to why Hartshorne has so persistently and voluminously worried about the Ontological Argument. Much more is at stake than the formal validity of a logical exercise. Instead, an entire metaphysical method, ultimately perhaps an entire way of life, is epitomized in this one proof. Destruction of the Ontological Argument, I would suggest, is tantamount for Hartshorne to the denial of philosophy as he conceives it.[22]

Before leaving this subject, it is worth glancing more closely at Hartshorne's argument in the dissertation, which consists of three "phases." The First Phase is a rather obscure statement of the view that God's existence is *a se* and that God cannot even be conceived not to exist: "The conception of the non-existence of that which is to exist, if at all, only in and of itself,—as a self-sustained, or self-existent being,—involves a contradiction" (OD 264). Hartshorne then goes on to specify aseity in terms of spontaneous self-exercised power, even going so far as to affirm a position he later condemns, that "Perfection is perfectly and eternally exercised power—is pure and inalienable actuality—actus purus" (OD 266). The conclusion of this phase is that "either the self-existent must be regarded as existent and the ground of all existence, or it must be regarded as an ideal fundamentally meaningless and contradictory" (OD 268f).

---

[22] Closely connected with this point is Hartshorne's affirmation in the dissertation that the conclusion of the ontological argument is no mere abstract proposition which makes no difference in our lives. Instead, "our idea of God is not merely *our* imperfect conception, but involves the Immanent self-consciousness of God, and so is able to mean this perfect reality by the latter's own aid—otherwise it could not; which is a form of the [ontological] proof" (OD 264n1). Such a statement suggests that Hartshorne's "neo-classical" proofs are deeply neo-Hegelian in spirit.

Hartshorne then offers important replies to three objections: (1) It is ridiculous, he says, to claim that necessity of thought does not mean the same as necessity of existence, for this would mean that what we must think to be the case we could nevertheless suppose not to be so, which is a contradiction. (Such "irrelevant nonsense," Hartshorne contends, should not be confused with contending that the idea of existence *a se* itself does not make sense—"the primary and most rational objection of Kant" [OD 270].) (2) Does the argument "leap" from idea to reality? Here Hartshorne takes a tack reminiscent of Descartes' Third Meditation. *No* idea, he says, can help but refer to (or "imply") some reality other than itself. All thought is *of* something other than itself. Therefore, since *all* consciousness leaps the "gulf" between ideality and reality, our thought of perfection cannot be our thought of our thought; if consistent, it cannot fail to be our thought of perfection. (3) What about concepts of fictitious or nonexistent entities? Here Hartshorne affirms something that is crucial to his life-long understanding of divinity: *"No finite individual, in its qualitative uniqueness or inner individuality, can be conceived"* (OD 271). No particular dragon but only *a* dragon—some dragon or other—is conceivable in full. Finite entities are individuated (for us, at least) not through the addition of determinations or universals (including, Hartshorne adds, space and time), but only through being actual or possible data of (our) perception. But Perfection or Divinity is a "quality" or property which only one individual *can* possess (and, Hartshorne somewhat obscurely adds, "possess" not in the sense of being an instance of a universal but rather in the sense of being the self-existent "Life" of that principle) (OD 273).

The Second Phase connects the notions of personality and life (including knowledge and value) with that of existence *a se*: "A Perfect Personality can only be conceived as a wholly self-controlled and self-existent Being" (OD 273). A "Perfect Personality" is one with all defects in knowledge, good-will and power removed: God must have "a perfect penetration and comprehensiveness of insight, a complete direct vision of all beings; a perfect sympathy and good-will toward all; and an unlimited power to assist them" (OD 275). This, Hartshorne affirms, is the ideal of friendship: "the Perfect Person is a mind who wills the good of all, embraces all in his sympathetic insight, and who contains the being of all in the circle of his own might" (OD 275). Since value is "pre-eminently generous and comprehending social intercourse" (OD 277), the ideal good is "the Perfect Friend" or "the Perfect Lover" (OD 277).

Phase Three argues for a premise upon which the first two phases depend—whether or not the idea of a "Perfect Personality" (and hence of existence *a se*) is consistent. Hartshorne contends that "the consistency of the idea of a Perfect Personality is implied in the rationality or consistency of thought in general or in any given case. . . . Our whole thesis has endeavored to demonstrate this" (OD 279). The ontological argument is therefore an entire metaphysics in miniature. One may argue from any of the ultimate categories of thought and being, but the result will always be the same: only an absolute One, inescapably conceived in personalistic terms, can give them "full and fundamental meaning" (OD 281). The claim is enormous: insofar as the concept of Perfection is inconsistent and confused, so also is "all thought and all life" without meaning. Life is literally without sense unless "Perfection" makes sense.

Although Hartshorne called this three-phase argument an "incomparably brilliant and cogent course of reasoning" at the time (OD 259), in 1965 he was prompted to say:

> I now think that both the standard criticisms and the older defences, including mine forty years ago, are all seriously—even disgracefully—defective. In 1923 I had, like so many others, failed to read Anselm with scholarly care; and I certainly took my self-appointed task of rebutting Kant far too casually. (AD ix)

Nevertheless, while the differences in Hartshorne's understanding of the ontological argument between the dissertation and *Anselm's Discovery* are great, they are considerably less than Hartshorne's language might indicate. Hartshorne does not say what defects he has in mind (the remarks about Anselm and Kant are of little help), but certainly he does not reject the metaphysical project of Phase Three, which is essentially the "global proof" of *Creative Synthesis and Philosophic Method*. Nor does he ever reject the connection, made in Phase One, between the possibility or conceivability of divine existence and its necessity. Nor does he ever shrink from affirming that Perfection must be personal (the gist of Phase Two). Where then are the defects? It would be absurdly superficial to say that Hartshorne's dissertation lacks the language and rigor of modern (especially modal) logic. Instead, the chief defect Hartshorne now finds in his dissertation, I would suggest, is its inadequate concept of Perfection, not its method of argumentation (cf. Section VI below).

V.

We turn now to some important metaphysical doctrines affirmed in the dissertation. For reasons of space we concentrate on the doctrines of experience, idealism (or psychicalism) and relations.

A. Experience, Hartshorne asserts at length, is necessarily and always both social and valuational. It is social in at least the sense that the objects of knowledge (or cognitive experience) are given to and are not constituted by the act of knowing (cf OD 202).

> Knowledge rests upon a unity of direct awareness *inclusive of objects and their actual natures*. Objects, not copies or representations of objects, are given or printed . . . . To deny the direct givenness of genuine existents is in principle fatal to knowledge. (OD 212, 214)

In "consciousness or awareness in general, . . . there is always *an other* directly involved and thus solipsism or subjectivism is avoided" (OD 220).

Since Hartshorne tends here (as later) to merge or equate knowledge with perception (cf OD 219), perceptual experience is likewise "social." Experience of the past, or memory, is also "social," for "If our thought does not embrace the past in its very pastness, we do not think the past" (OD 205n1). Since knowledge, perception and memory are, for him, quite evidently "social," Hartshorne seems to conclude (justifiably or not) that *all* experience is "social." *All* experience is experience *of* something given to and not constituted by the experience itself. This "of" relation is the embryonic form of Hartshorne's later doctrine of "inclusion," which he tends to describe in the language of Whitehead's doctrine of "prehension." But one must beware of reading too much of a fully social doctrine of prehension into the dissertation. It, after all, is a defense of *Monism*, and Hartshorne aims to show that all things are included in the One or Divine Good. What chiefly vitiates a fully social doctrine of inclusion here is the lack of any event ontology, of a theory concerning just what the fundamental entities are between which the metaphysical relation of "inclusion" holds. This lack is evident in the following quotations, where Hartshorne apparently conceives the relation of inclusion as holding not between events or states of enduring individuals but between the individuals themselves:

> Dependence of one *being* upon another is conceivable solely as an *identity* of being, so that a change of state in the one has, as its logically inevitable aspect, a change in the other. (OD 36; emphasis added).

> The spiritual view of unity and wholeness is alone capable of comprehending [including?] in a genuine "in" relation, the whole of experience and its contents. (OD 191).

One possible reason for Hartshorne's confusion (or at least ambiguity) here is his apparent desire to make the entire value relation—though not the knowledge relation—internal to the given objects of experience. The mind as knower unifies its objects but does not constitute (is not internal to) them qua objects of knowledge; but the mind as valuer (at least in the case of God) *is* supposed to constitute what it values (cf OD 41). But if the value relation is constitutive, so must be the knowledge relation, since knowledge is conceivable only in valuational terms, according to Hartshorne (cf. below).

Experience is not only social but also valuational.[23] Value, for Harts-

---

[23] The roots of Hartshorne's theodicy lie in his belief that value is a categorial feature of experience. If all value is finally aesthetic in character, then "nothing is wholly unbeautiful," and what *we* call "beautiful" things are only especially beautiful things. Ugliness is then explained (following Bosanquet, Hartshorne indicates) as a conflict of elements possessing intrinsic value; it is not possible for there to be a *total* absence of beauty (OD 233-35). This position permits two slightly different ways of explaining non-aesthetic dis-value or evil: (1) If all value is in the end aesthetic, then non-aesthetic evil is explicable in terms of aesthetic evil, i.e., ugliness. (2) Whether or not all value *is* aesthetic, if all evil involves conflict or disharmony of intrinsically valuable elements, then non-aesthetic as well as aesthetic evil will be explicable in the same way. Hartshorne holds both views, believing that the "conflict" or "disharmony" which is the root of all evil in (2) is precisely aesthetic in character as in (1).

horne, "is essentially social, a matter of co-enjoyment, willed and felt as such" (OD 220). Value is neither "a shorthand term for a peculiar neutrally describable complex" (OD 221) nor "a merely subjective element or activity of pleasure" (OD 223) but rather "implies worth in the object in substantially the same sense as the experience itself possesses worth" (OD 233). That is, our experience is pervaded by value, both in its subjective aspect (for our experience as a whole is more or less valuable) and in its objective aspect (for the given elements in our experience are themselves other experiences which are valuable in the same sense, though perhaps in different degrees, as our own experience is valuable).

Hartshorne is quite prepared to extend the meaning of "value" to coincide with that of "being"; this is the core of his major idealistic argument: being entails experience; experience entails social relation; social relation entails value; hence being entails value. It is only a slight exaggeration to say that this schema represents the entirety of the dissertation, the central thesis of which is that what is can be understood only in terms of value (and value's implicit absolute standard, the Divine Good or Perfect Being). The persistence of being as coincident with value in Hartshorne's later thought helps us to understand his difference of opinion with Whitehead on "perishing."[24] For Hartshorne, nothing real is "lost" in "perishing" (which he tends to regard as more a metaphor than a philosophical doctrine). The reason is that for him what is, reality, or being as such, is precisely equivalent to its value in and for—i.e., its being included in the experience of—the One. If God did not include in His experience all that a thing is—if something, such as "subjective immediacy," were inevitably "lost" to His experience—then in Hartshorne's view what is omitted could not be real. What something really is it is to "a perfected Beneficient Interest"; it is present in its entirety, "with all its qualities." "What the man really is, *that* he must be to the perfect appraisal, or to the perfect friend" (OD 1d; cf 109). The same conclusion follows, Hartshorne believes, from the admission that value is in principle social. If everything that is, is valuable, and what is valuable is in principle shareable, and if God experiences or values everything that can be valued, then everything that *is* not only can be but also must be experienced by God (cf OD 6d, 223f, 233f). In the language of Hartshorne's dissertation, there must be a "common element" between an object within and without the mind, which can only be "an Ultimate Valuation or Self-significance *realizing an identical phase of itself in both the mind and the object"* (OD 243).[25] In sum, Hartshorne wishes to urge (in agreement with Whitehead) that something can become an element of one's

<hr />

[24] To be sure, Hartshorne believes—wrongly, I think—that this difference is more apparent than real.

[25] Hartshorne hastens to add that God is not the *only* creator of value; individual experients create the new values of their own experiences, though not of the objects of their experiences. Still, the value of both subject and objects must relate to a standard valuation which includes both subject's and objects' values and compares them in its own terms (OD 243).

own experience without becoming *peculiar* to it, and further (here apparently parting company with Whitehead), that *nothing* is in principle (or in God) peculiar to *any* experience, not even that experience's own "subjective immediacy," individuality as such, or whatever.

Various consequences follow from Hartshorne's contention that all experience is valuational:

1. Since knowledge is ultimately empirical, it is also valuational in no merely intellectual sense. Removal of contradition is essential to fullness of value: "the attempt to overcome contraditions by adequate ideas may be viewed as really the attempt to attain a full realization of the essential values of experience and reality" (OD 18). Value is hence the key, Hartshorne believes, to solution of various outstanding epistemological difficulties.

2. Value is also the key to ontology, though usually neglected as such (OD 20). (We shall elaborate this point later.)

3. Value is hence the highest ultimate category or perhaps even above all categories whatsoever (cf OD 28, 248n1). Value retains its unique status in Hartshorne's later philosophy: unlike all other categories, value is never subject to the law of polarity, for its contrast term has no positive meaning; indeed, all "contrast" itself is a matter of degrees of value. In a real sense, therefore, "the Good" is not so much a super-category as something beyond all categories, in spite of Hartshorne's statement that value *is* a concept which "differs from other concepts only as a more completely self-conscious meaning differs from a less" (OD 200f).

4. If metaphysical categories are implied by "all life and thought," and if value is the supreme (or super-) category, then it would seem to follow that all terms are to varying degrees value terms. The "One Principle" is "present in every concept as an implicit meaning," though more explicit in some than in others (OD 50f), and this "One Principle" is valuational:

> For us all terms are fully grasped only as denoting value—the self-enjoying mind is the first and last principle of all its concepts. Every thing is good, but in varying degrees and manners. . . . all meanings for us are values. (OD 54, 55)

Further, since the final appeal in philosophy is to concrete experience, "The only way to know value is to enjoy it" (OD 54), so that knowledge of value is equivalent to realizing—and re-actualizing—values in conscious experience.

5. It follows from 4 that value cannot be reduced to fact, that value terms cannot be defined in terms of value-neutral terms. To buttress this contention, Hartshorne offers a version of G. E. Moore's argument against "naturalism," as follows: "Value [is] not a shorthand term for a peculiar neutrally describable complex," since given any such complex it is always proper to ask whether it is good (OD 222f, cf 189). But Hartshorne's conclusion from this argument is more sweeping than Moore's. Both men agree that value cannot be reduced to fact because it has more "content" (as Hartshorne puts it), but whereas Moore largely intuits the content, Harts-

horne goes on to explicate it in a metaphysical theory of experience as feeling of others' feelings. "Value is not verbal but is alone the essence of the real" (OD 200), and "Mind is, for us, essentially concerned with valuation" (OD 216). Thus Hartshorne's idealist ontology, to which we now turn, is not an instance of the "naturalistic fallacy" because "mind" is already a value-term.

B. "Teleological Monism" implies an ontology of experience: what is real is "measured" by divine experience; but "measurement" is possible only if the measured is of the same nature as the measurer; hence whatever is is of the nature of experience. Although Idealism (or psychicalism) is not the central thesis of the dissertation, Hartshorne nevertheless offers a number of arguments in its behalf:

1) In Hartshorne's view, even the "working principles," the methodological cornerstones of philosophy, are "best understood" on a valuational idealistic view (OD 67). Only Idealism can explain how knowledge is possible (for it alone accounts for the subject as well as for the object of knowledge), and only a valuational view can explain how consistency or the "harmony of meanings" is a criterion of truth (OD 64-66).

2) "Matter" is a set of "isolated entities" or an abstraction with meaning only in "the central activity or self-realization of mind" (OD 91). "Unmental Being" is "unthinkable" since we cannot know "anything outside our awareness"; our mind in some sense "includes" the universe, so that "Somehow all that is is present in our awareness, and it has no mode of being not exhaustively represented in terms of this relation" (OD 204f). However, solipsism or subjective idealism is *not* entailed, Hartshorne believes, since our awareness also includes the One, "so that our thought of 'all reality' is a partial realization on our part of the Embracing Thought." Since the One Mind "includes" all, "our concept of Reality rests at its core upon a Meaning, which does include whatever that concept intends to refer to or imply (OD 206). More simply put, the denial of matter does not entail solipsism due to the social character of experience.

3) In support of 2), Hartshorne urges that mental reality is "the sole initial certainty," while materialism and "neutralism" are dubitable. Thinking is "self-verifying," a "self-recording" "register." This argument from certainty is muted if not missing in Hartshorne's later writings, perhaps because here Hartshorne is too much the Cartesian rationalist exaggerating the clearly conscious aspects of experience. This exaggeration leads, for example, to the following claim which is quite at variance with Hartshorne's later panpsychism:

All objects are known to me only in so far as they become objects-to-me, and since parts of my organism, including the interior of my brain, are not so given—and might for aught I know certainly in any absolute sense be of a very different character than any theory holds them to be—such entities cannot constitute parts of "my experience," which, as individual and the basis for all my knowledge of individuality, is absolutely certain. (OD 197)

Hartshorne's later arguments for Idealism do not stress any alleged *immediate* self-certainty of the mind but rather the mediate, reflective, interpretative power of psychical as opposed to non-psychical categories. Idealism triumphs not in an initial flash of intuitive insight but in the long hard struggle to make sense out of all varieties of experience.

4) Thus Hartshorne's central argument for Idealism really occupies the whole volume: it is the attempt to show that "reality" or "being" has meaning only in terms of (valuational) experience, that to be real is equivalent in meaning to being related to mind—not finite but infinite or perfect mind. Our mind is a partial reflection of this equivalence, which enables us both to grasp the equivalence and also to realize that we do not constitute it. In Hartshorne's words, "The mind's intuition of itself, its self-significance, becomes the final and sole reference for all quality. Ultimately all meaning is in principle *fully* self-conscious" (OD 210). Here is another reason why Hartshorne's arguments for idealism terminate in, but do not begin with, a (partially?) certain grasp of the equivalence of being and mind: to *begin* (and perhaps to *end*) with this grasp in God's prerogative; we must *seek* to *approximate* it.

5) Hartshorne's dissertation also contains a version of an argument to which Hartshorne has recently devoted some further attention.[26] Human knowledge is always partial, unclear, vague, obscure. These limitations are "negations" of "what mind [as knower] essentially is"; "we are not all that the idea of mind [or knowledge] implies." Hence "Absolute [or divine] knowledge is only *knowledge* taken in the full and fundamental meaning of the term" (OD 281). Given that we know what "knowledge" means, and that we know that we do not adequately or "fully and fundamentally" exemplify that meaning, it follows, Hartshorne argues, that there must be a perfect knowledge whose scope, clarity and detail is coextensive with reality. In this way, "ideal knowledge defines reality."[27]

6) One argument which Hartshorne employs here is *not* used in his later writings, for reasons which point up one of the fundamental defects of the dissertation. Hartshorne asserts that not only is the relation of Being "wholly internal to all things," "a relation without which a thing is nothing," but it is also "manifestly that which endows it [the thing which has the relation] with all that it has" (OD 113). Being (and hence all its later, more concrete categorial specifications such as knowledge and value) is "a wholly concrete principle" because it is "constitutive" and hence totally creative of everything. This is Hartshorne's dissertation doctrine of the "concrete universal," which will receive fuller treatment below. Here we need merely note the elementary logical error Hartshorne commits when he

[26] See "Ideal Knowledge Defines Reality: What Was True in 'Idealism'," *Journal of Philosophy* 43 (October 10, 1946), 573-82; "Letter," *Journal of Philosophy* 43 (December 19, 1946), 724; "Idealism and Our Experience of Nature," pp. 70-80; and "The Case for Idealism," *Philosophical Forum* 1 (1968), 7-23.

[27] The title of the first article cited in the last footnote.

says that "A relation without which its term is literally nothing is a contradiction unless the thing is *all* that it is by virtue of the relation" (OD 114). A relation "without which its term is literally nothing" is certainly *necessary* for that term, but how does it follow that it is sufficient or *constitutive*, that it is "*all*" that the term is? Hartshorne here affirms a doctrine which he later rejects or at least severely modifies, that the highest universal is supremely concrete instead of supremely abstract. Recognition of the logical error we have pointed out may have played a role in Hartshorne's rejection of the doctrine of the concrete universal; in any case this particular argument for Idealism makes no further appearance in his writings.

C. Section Nine, which is explicitly devoted to the subject of relations, contains an interesting, if undeveloped, version of Hartshorne's later doctrine of polarity. Nearly all of Section Nine argues that external or "noncontributory" relations imply an "underlying reality" to "mediate" them. Hartshorne tries to show that a pluralism of "independent entities pervaded by no common life" but related only by relations is untenable. Instead, all elements of experience are "manifestly" pervaded by a common principle of "all alike possessing meaning and meaning for one and the same apprehending mind" (OD 150). Things are related not simply by relations but also by an encompassing mind (just as inferences do not themselves infer); to relate is a function requiring a relating agent, which is ultimately the divine mind (OD 151).

Whatever validity these arguments possess is perhaps less important than what Hartshorne's purpose is in using them. His aim is to show that a world of purely externally-related entities is an absurdity and that any conceivable world requires both internal *and* external relations. "The *internal* nature of a thing is its value to the One," so that what it essentially is involves relation to the One, while *external* relations "are aspects of its status to the One, not as directly valuable but as fulfilling a purpose in relation to a larger whole or unit of value" (OD 151f). The only conceivable way of accounting for both internal and external relations, Hartshorne believes, is to conceive of all relations of a thing as "contained" in a "mediating Reality"; all properties, he suggests, are relational, at least in the sense of being modes of relatedness or worth to the One (OD 165, cf 152n1). What is important to note is that even though Hartshorne's Monism seems to favor internal relations (all relations are internal to the One), nevertheless he emphasizes that both internal and external relations are required *and* that only a modified monistic view can account for this requirement. There is a double implication here: on the one hand, neither term of a categorial pair has meaning unless its partner also has independent and contrastive meaning (Hartshorne's later Law of Polarity).[28] On the other hand, the instances (in this case only God, but later every actuality) of one of the con-

---

[28] The Law of Polarity is also suggested in the following passage: "The distinction of whole and its parts and relations must be maintained or both terms vanish" (OD 123).

trastive terms "includes" or "contains" the instances of the others and thus the whole contrast (the Law of Inclusion). Neither doctrine or "Law," however, is very fully developed here; their development may well be one of the products of Whitehead's influence on Hartshorne.

VI.

Our final topic is the doctrine of God developed here. In an important sense, the whole dissertation is a single ramified argument for God's existence. Metaphysical philosophy and natural theology so nearly coincide in method, sources and conclusions, that one could express its intended result by saying either that it is an adequate system of metaphysical categories or that it is an adequate doctrine of God. Thus far, it is simply a precursor of Hartshorne's later philosophy. But there is a profound difference between the doctrine of God in the dissertation and the doctrine of God in Hartshorne's later philosophy, a difference which *may* mark the extent of Whitehead's influence upon Hartshorne. In spite of what Hartshorne has recently implied,[29] there is no clear conception of a dipolar God in the dissertation. Hartshorne does insist here on the freedom of the creatures in relation to their creator and on the personality (love, knowledge, valuation) of God. Yet all internal evidence indicates that, as of 1923, Hartshorne had not fully, or not clearly, broken away from the traditional conception of an *actus purus* or monopolar God.

It must be admitted at once that Hartshorne does say many things here which in a later context would be ascribed to God's concrete consequent nature. For instance, in defining his variety of monism on the very first page, Hartshorne speaks of the conception "that all things have their being and nature in terms of one Ultimate Being, one 'all-general and all-sufficient principle' or 'World-Ground'" (OD 1). What is this "all-sufficient principle"? It is not, Hartshorne insists, an "all-devouring" Absolute which strips finite entities of freedom and being by making them adjectives, appearances or phases of the One (OD 2). Further, "we do not believe that Monism has any force to establish the existence of a Being unrelated to change" (OD 2; cf 185, 277, 300). The "all-sufficient principle" cannot be aloof from concrete process. Neither can it determine all action, for to do so would make all action its action (OD 3). Instead, it is "a single register upon which all facts are inscribed, a mirror in which all things are reflected and must be so reflected in order to be" (OD 4, emphasis omitted). Hartshorne is determined to contrast his "Personalistic" or qualified Monism with "Absolutistic" or "all-devouring" Monism (OD 4). "Everything qualifies or makes a difference to the One," but everything is of significance for others (including the One) only by being of significance for itself (OD 3).

Nevertheless, in spite of Hartshorne's protestations on behalf of a qualified monism, there are overwhelming indications of a stronger absolutistic

---

[29] "The Development of My Philosophy," p. 217.

tendency in the dissertation. Nor are these indications confined to isolated passages, such as the following: "Perfection is perfectly and eternally exercised power—is pure and inalienable actuality—actus purus" (OD 266). Rather, the tendency is an integral part of its argument, as the following three examples help to show.

(1) Hartshorne insists that the One (or God) is not identical with the Absolute (or "the totality of all that is"); the One is rather "the *principle* through which the totalization of the items in His identity as the Ultimate Person, must be thought" (OD 7, emphasis added). But what is the status of this "principle"? In a long discussion entitled "Alleged Abstractness of the Ultimate Universals" (i.e., of metaphysical categories), Hartshorne argues that such a principle is supremely concrete, not supremely abstract (as in his later philosophy). The "higher universals" manifest themselves in a variety of lower universals without losing their self-identity and without becoming formless and indeterminate. For example, the concept-universal of color "contains"—at least "implicitly"—that of blue: "In order to be blue, a thing must so far reject green and red, but to possess color as such would be to possess *all* colors in such a way that the possession of one offers no bar to the possession of another" (OD 42). Hartshorne admits that no doubt the "ordinary understanding" thinks that universals are abstract, but such understanding is valid only for ordinary purposes and not for philosophical ones. The ordinary understanding is concerned with the "consequences in [individual] *practical sensuous* experience" and for it "the real is what makes a difference in terms of the interests we have in hand" (this is Hartshorne's view of the limited usefulness of Pragmatism) (OD 45). But for philosophy, "the reality of things is more than their relation to us, as possible contents of our finite experience" (OD 45f). Philosophy transcends ordinary purposes to enjoy "self-absorption in the truth." In this rarified atmosphere, categorial universals are not emptily abstract but fully concrete (OD 46). From such a lofty vantage point, Hartshorne can speak of the One as at once a "principle" *and* a "Being" which "includes the finite beings, not as instances of the class Perfection or Ultimateness, as 'animal' includes dog and horse, but includes them by owning them, by their entering into Its Life and being of *value* there" (OD 50).

From the standpoint of Hartshorne's later philosophy, of course, it is quite wrong to conflate the inclusiveness of abstract concepts with the inclusiveness of concrete individuals. What is chiefly lacking here, I would suggest, is (a) a full-fledged doctrine of inclusion which does not conflate concrete and abstract entities, and (b) Hartshorne's later doctrine of the dipolar "Categorial Individual," whose unique individuality (and existence) is *entailed by* its categorial description, but whose full individuality or particularity is not *identical with* that description. The description (God's eternal essence or Primordial Nature) is abstract, and the particularity (His changing actuality or Consequent States) is concrete, even though the abstract description entails that there must always be *some* concrete instance of itself.

(2) A similar confusion arises in Hartshorne's discussion of the meaning of "part" and "whole." In his later philosophy, Hartshorne uses these terms to express his doctrine of inclusion: if A includes B then B is a part of A. Here, however, a whole is defined as "an organized aggregate of entities," called its parts (OD 5). Hartshorne then insists that a clear distinction must be made between the whole of things ("the organized totality of all beings") and the "Ultimate One" ("the sustaining and organizing principle of the very totality in which it occurs itself as a member") (OD 5). Yet this "principle" is supposed to be constitutive of both parts and whole; only by being "included" (in some sense) in the One, does the totality exist or have being. Hartshorne concludes with the following problematic statement:

> Since all things are in God and God is in himself, the Absolute Totality of reals is comprehended in God—not as a member of a further, more inclusive system, but as the objective scope of the Divine self-possessed Life. God sustains in his being the system of which he is himself a member, and his inclusion as a member in that system is one with his self-inclusion of himself in it. And the comprehension of the system in God is just his holding and sustaining it within his own life. (OD 6)

This passage is notably unclear as to the relative status of the "Absolute Totality" and the "Divine Life," especially as regards concreteness and abstractness. Hartshorne apparently wants the "Divine Life" to be both an abstract principle and a concrete existence. But according to his later philosophy, the same thing cannot be supremely both in the same respect. Hartshorne's unclarity here clouds the sense in which one thing "includes" another, even though there are glimpses of his later position in the (at least verbal) distinction between "Absolute Totality" and "Divine Life."

(3) In Section Six, "The Argument from the Category of Being," Hartshorne holds that Being is "a one something the relation to which of having being is wholly internal to all things" (OD 113). It follows, he believes, that "a relation [such as that to Being] without which a thing is *nothing*, is manifestly that which endows it with *all* that it has" (OD 113, emphasis added). Hence Being is "a wholly concrete principle since it is "constitutive" and "creative" (OD 114).[30]

We have already noted the invalidity of arguing from "a relation without which a thing is nothing" to "a relation which endows a thing with all that it has." From the fact that the absence of A entails the absence of B (where A is necessary for B), it simply does not follow that the presence of A entails the presence of B in all its concreteness (where A is sufficient for or constitutive of B). Hartshorne seems to vacillate here between treating the One as a universal principle necessary to everything (but hence abstract)

---

[30] See Hartshorne's earlier statement that Being "must be admitted to register and account for and even to contribute *all*: inasmuch as the removal of this aspect is one with the removal of all" (OD 104).

and treating it as constitutive of everything (hence concrete). At times he seems to believe that concreteness is itself concrete or even the most concrete. This confusion might be rectified as follows from Hartshorne's later standpoint: one *may* say both that the One is included in anything possible and actual (is necessary but abstract) and that the One includes everything both actual and possible (is concrete and may be contingent if its content is contingent). *But* one cannot say both things of the One *in the same respect* (as regards the concrete/abstract distinction). No doubt *the fact that* the One includes everything both actual and possible is necessary (in Hartshorne's philosophy, at any rate), but this fact is only an abstract "part" included in the concrete One. Inclusion-by-the-One is constitutive of the being of anything, Hartshorne continues to affirm, but this "being" is not its full concrete *actuality* but its *existence*, the *fact* of its being an actuality. Failure to make such distinctions are what chiefly render his early doctrine of God radically confused or plainly inconsistent with his later views.

Hartshorne's early unclarity or confusion concerning the nature of God has various ramifications. Perhaps the most important concern the freedom of the creatures and Hartshorne's attempted theodicy. Hartshorne is adamant that his valuational monism does not entail determinism: "the One, although all-powerful, must not determine each act of the creature" (OD 29). Nevertheless, his reasons why determinism is not entailed are importantly at variance with his later position. Omnipotence, he argues in the dissertation, "has to" provide for other autonomous individuals in order to "watch over" their development; there must be

> a voluntary self-limitation of the Perfect Control over finite beings to some extent in order that those beings may not be entirely extinguished (since their identity as separate beings depends upon their reality as agents) as distinct entities. (OD 29, emphasis omitted)

God's control, Hartshorne says, is "limited" *voluntarily*, as "a reasonable exercise of infinitely good Omnipotence" (OD 29). Still, there is the suggestion that God *need not* have so limited himself, that the mere existence of some creatures or other is only contingent (upon God's free decision to create them). Every finite act "must carry with it" the Divine Act so that God has always at least potential (total) control over everything; it is up to him whether or not to *allow* some "finitely originated deflection" *if* He wants to continue any and every finite agent in being (OD 30). Such a position Hartshorne later repudiates. He would find contradictory or confused the statement in the dissertation that the creatures' relation to God is "an utter dependence which allows the exercise of freedom" (OD 31).

Unclarity is also evident in Hartshorne's reply to Schiller's challenge that the monistic God has no social relations and no interest in anything except itself (since it lacks nothing). Hartshorne replies that this is "careless and loose thinking," based on the false premise that God must have all goodness in Himself "as a self-enclosed and solitary consciousness" instead of being a loving God who expresses Himself in a world of creatures

(OD 276). But this reply is quickly undermined by Hartshorne's contention that an "absolute" can, if it wishes, limit itself to make room for creaturely freedom (OD 276). In brief, Hartshorne makes creaturely freedom not a categorial (metaphysical) requirement binding even upon divinity, but rather the result of a free and quite contingent decision by God (no matter how much it is "in character"). Hartshorne's later philosophy removes this lingering possibility of divine fiat.

Theodicy is another casualty of the same confusion. Hartshorne's general and abiding theodicy is that evil is the inevitable by-product of free creaturely decisions; to ensure their free existence as more than adjectives of God, the creatures must have a "power of self-determination." "Now if the One Being determined all completely, all alleged thinkers, agents, wills, are really *nothing but* manifestations of the One Will, and *are* simply the One, seen truly and fully" (OD 250). Such a view requires that "no Being *could* guarantee the actions of created beings or determine them to be always good" (OD 251, emphasis added). But in the dissertation Hartshorne leaves open the possibility that God might not have created free creatures at all; he asserts merely that *if* God wants such-and-such a world (which of course, considering his loving nature, he does as a matter of fact want), *then* he must relinquish complete control. There remains the *logical* possibility that God could have created a world entirely devoid of freedom, or even need not have created at all. Even though Hartshorne is not always clear on this point, [31] divine voluntarism (or contingency of creation) seems to have the last word, a position which Hartshorne later clearly repudiates.

The gap between the "concrete universal" of the early philosophy and Hartshorne's later "categorial individual," while great, is measured by only a few interlocked doctrines. The One of the dissertation is both concrete and universal; quite obviously universality is not yet connected with abstractness. The connection is not made, I would suggest, because two key (and correlative) doctrines, in their full-fledged form at any rate, are lacking here: (a) There is no doctrine of inclusion, of which the particular/universal relation is later treated as an instance by Hartshorne.[32] Hence there is no clear connection of the way in which "higher" universals such as color are related to "lower" universals such as blue with the way in which par-

---

[31] For example, he says that "Freedom, choice, responsibility, chance of error—all belong, is our contention, to *any* world, *as capable of being consistently thought*" (OD 253, emphasis added).

[32] The relevant part of Hartshorne's doctrine of inclusion may be summed up as follows: If *a* includes *b*, then

   (1) *a* strictly implies *b;*
   (2) it cannot be the case that *a* is a universal and *b* a particular;
   (3) if both *a* and *b* are universals, then *a* must be more determinate or definite than *b;*
   (4) if both *a* and *b* are particulars, then *b* cannot be the successor of *a.*

Hartshorne's dissertation utilizes (1) and (3), but forgets (2)—so that, for example, the universal "blue" cannot include particular blue things. Also Hartshorne later rejects the early belief that "color" is more determinate than "blue."

ticulars include universals. The doctrine of the concrete universal is perhaps the chief instance of a legacy from Idealism which Hartshorne later dropped; such a rejection, however, is the exception and not the rule. (b) There is no event-ontology, so that Hartshorne fails to see that inclusion holds most basically (most concretely) not between temporally enduring individuals but between momentary states of enduring individuals. Among its various ramifications, lack of an event-ontology prevents distinguishing God's essence (the more or less abstract principle of individuality) from His existence (the concrete actualization of that principle).

The source and occasion of these additions (inclusion and event-ontology) to the early positions is another matter. *That* they are not there present, or present only in a confused form, is patent; *how* Hartshorne later acquired them is not totally clear, although Whitehead undoubtedly played a great role.

VII.

In summary, close consideration of Hartshorne's dissertation indicates that most of his mature philosophy was developed independently of, because prior to, his contact with Whitehead (and Peirce). Only in his doctrine of God do significant ambiguities emerge which were later clarified in Whiteheadian terms. Even here, however, it is arguable that Whitehead's influence has consisted not so much in altering as in clarifying Hartshorne's antecedent beliefs, thereby furthering Hartshorne's initial and never relinquished convictions concerning the nature, purpose, method and general conclusions of metaphysical philosophy. One can only agree with Hartshorne that his relation to Whitehead is certainly not one of "intellectual descent" but more like one of "pre-established harmony."[33]

[33] "The Development of My Philosophy," p. 222.

CHAPTER III

Hartshorne's Differences from Whitehead

DAVID R. GRIFFIN

Alfred North Whitehead and Charles Hartshorne are often mentioned in one breath, as if they represented a single viewpoint. And there is much justification for this. But there are also important differences between their philosophical views. The purpose of this paper is to list and discuss the major differences to which Hartshorne himself has called attention. They fall under two major categories: the nature of possibility, and the nature of actuality. And most of them involve the relation of possibility or finite actuality to God.

I THE NATURE OF POSSIBILITY

1. *The Divine Dipolarity.* Although Hartshorne suggests that Whitehead has made the greatest contribution to theism in centuries,[1] he holds that Whitehead's doctrine of God involves serious confusions and inconsistencies with his own metaphysical principles.

Both men agree that God is dipolar. Hartshorne refers to the two poles as God's "abstract essence" and "concrete states." Whitehead names them the "primordial nature" and "consequent nature." From some of Hartshorne's statements one might infer that the two conceptions of dipolarity were identical.[2] But they are not. For Whitehead, God is a single actual entity. Hence the divine dipolarity must be that of an actual entity. "Analogously to all actual entities, the nature of God is dipolar. He has a primordial nature and a consequent nature."[3] The primordial nature is analogous to the conceptual pole of an actual occasion, while the consequent nature

---

[1] *Philosophers Speak of God,* p. 273. Hereafter, PSG.

[2] Hartshorne often remarks that Whitehead would have expressed his own meaning better had he spoken of consequent "states" instead of a consequent "nature": "Whitehead's Metaphysics," p. 32 in *Whitehead and the Modern World,* by Victor Lowe, Charles Hartshorne, and A. H. Johnson (Boston: Beacon Press, 1950); reprinted in *Whitehead's Philosophy: Selected Essays, 1935-1970,* p. 13 (hereafter, WP). See also "Whitehead and Contemporary Philosophy," p. 42 (WP 159) in *The Relevance of Whitehead,* ed. Ivor Leclerc (London: Allen and Unwin, 1961). He stresses that Whitehead spoke of the primordial nature as a mere abstraction, deficient in actuality: "Whitehead and Contemporary Philosophy," pp. 24, 37 (WP 144, 155); *Reality as Social Process,* p. 203 (hereafter, RSP); PSG 270, 276, 287, 310. And some of Hartshorne's remarks suggest that the primordial nature is what he himself calls the abstract essence of God (RSP 199, 202f).

[3] *Process and Reality,* p. 524 (hereafter, PR).

corresponds to the physical pole, so that in God the conceptual pole precedes the physical.[4]

For Hartshorne, the doctrine that God is a single actual entity involves serious mistakes. His general criticism is that it seems to make God an exception to the metaphysical principles, which Whitehead himself said should be avoided.[5] Partly to avoid this, Hartshorne says God should be regarded as a "living person," i.e., a personally-ordered society of occasions of experience. The two poles of God's reality cannot therefore be understood as analogous to the physical and mental poles of a finite occasion (although each divine occasion can be understood as dipolar in this sense), but as analogous to the distinction between a man's enduring character, on the one hand, and the concrete states of his existence which instantiate this abstract character, on the other. (Of course, the man's character is contingent, and only relatively time-independent, whereas God's character or essence is necessary and absolutely independent.)[6] Accordingly, Hartshorne will not follow Whitehead in describing God's unchanging pole as simply "conceptual"; for it is "at once conceptual, volitional, and perceptual," being "the *common element of all the successive conceptual, perceptual, and appetitive states of the divine life,* abstracting from the differences between these states."[7]

In passing it should be noted that, after so many years of defending the idea of God as a personally-ordered society, Hartshorne has recently suggested a possible modification: God is perhaps "a society of societies, a multiplicity of persons—somewhat . . . analogous to classical trinitarian views."[8] This thinking is motivated by the problem of combining relativity physics, which seems to deny a cosmic "now," with the idea of a single strand of divine occasions, each of which implies a "now" with a settled past and an open future (CSPM 123ff, 291). This revised view would mean that one cannot speak of "God now," but only of "God here-now," which would not be "the same concrete reality as God somewhere else 'now'." On this view "the simple analogy with human consciousness as a single

---

[4] PR 54, 134, 528.

[5] "Interrogation of Charles Hartshorne," p. 324 in *Philosophical Interrogations,* ed. Sydney and Beatrice Rome (New York: Holt, Rinehart and Winston, 1964); "From Colonial Beginnings to Philosophical Greatness," *The Monist* 48/3 (July, 1964), 327f; "Whitehead's Novel Intuition," p. 23 (WP 166) in *Alfred North Whitehead: Essays on His Philosophy,* ed. George L. Kline (Englewood Cliffs: Prentice-Hall, 1963); and *Creative Synthesis and Philosophic Method,* p. xv (hereafter, CSPM). For a discussion of the exceptions Hartshorne probably has in mind, see John B. Cobb, Jr., *A Christian Natural Theology* (Philadelphia: Westminster, 1965), pp. 185-90.

[6] "Whitehead's Idea of God," pp. 530f (WP 75) in *The Philosophy of Alfred North Whitehead:* The Library of Living Philosophers, ed. Paul A. Schilpp (Evanston and Chicago: Northwestern University Press, 1941).

[7] *Ibid.*

[8] "Whitehead in French Perspective: A Review Article," *The Thomist* 33/3 (July, 1969), 578. Cf. "Whitehead and Ordinary Language," *The Southern Journal of Philosophy* 7/4 (Winter, 1969-70), 442 (WP 178).

linear succession of states collapses" (CSPM 123f). Hartshorne has mixed feelings about this view, and still seems to lean more to his older view that physics, which deals with reality from the standpoint of localized observers, it cannot settle the question as to whether there might be a cosmic simultaneity for a non-localized or ubiquitous subject, a simultaneity which would not be identical with the perspectives of any of the finite entities.[9] However, if Hartshorne were to adopt the idea of God as a society of societies, I am not sure that his view would differ substantively from Lewis Ford's reworking of William Christian's position that God is *an* actual entity. Ford has conceived God as an everlasting concrescence who never has a unified prehension of the universe from a spatially all-inclusive perspective, but who always prehends reality from every perspective, prehending from each spatiotemporal locus only what can be prehended from there, so that God's prehension of an event at one point would not involve the prehension of a contemporary of that event.[10]

2. *Eternal Possibilities.* Whitehead believes in many eternal realities. However these should be understood to be related, one can at least distinguish verbally the metaphysical categories, the primordial nature of God, and eternal objects ("pure possibilities") of the objective and subjective species. Hartshorne does not affirm so much eternal possibility. The aspect of Whitehead's view with which he most explicitly takes issue is the doctrine of eternal objects. He believes that potentialities should be divided into two radically different levels: (1) the metaphysical categories, the completely general dimensions of reality without which nothing can be genuinely conceived, and (2) the specific qualities, those which need not be instantiated in every experience, and from which one can therefore abstract and still have meaning.[11] Only the former are eternal.

However, Hartshorne allows that mathematical ideas ("numbers or similarly abstract entities") might also be eternal, since they are extremely abstract and general, and arithmetic and pure geometry probably follow from the categories of logic.[12] Since Whitehead referred to the objective species of eternal objects as "mathematical platonic forms," it appears that Hartshorne's objection to the doctrine of eternal objects is restricted primarily to the subjective species, those which can contribute to the subjective form of a prehension as well as its objective datum (PR 446). He believes it a serious mistake to speak of this qualitative possibility as a multitude of eternally distinct, determinate entities with their individual identities.[13] General qualitative possibility should be regarded instead as

[9] CSPM 17, 53f, 123, 125; "Interrogation of Charles Hartshorne," p. 325.

[10] Lewis S. Ford, "Is Process Theism Compatible with Relativity Theory?" *The Journal of Religion* 48/2 (April, 1968), 131-34.

[11] "Whitehead's Idea of God," p. 557 (WP 96); CSPM 59, 67f, 121f.

[12] *The Logic of Perfection,* p. 94 (hereafter, LP); CSPM 66f; "Whitehead's Idea of God," pp. 557f (WP 97).

[13] Throughout the following discussion the reader will note that Hartshorne equates "definiteness" and "determinateness." But Whitehead distinguishes them, applying the

an "affective continuum," in which subdivisions can be inexhaustibly created, and which is hence "beyond multitude."[14] Hartshorne believes Whitehead to have violated his own insight that "definiteness is the soul of actuality"[15] by speaking of eternal objects as "forms of definiteness." The actual or concrete is finite and atomic; the possible or abstract is an infinite continuum.[16]

Accordingly, Hartshorne eschews Whitehead's term "eternal objects," and returns to the traditional term "universals." He believes the term "eternal objects" begs the question as to whether there are, besides universals which are absolutely time-independent (the metaphysical categories), some which are only relatively so. Some might suspect that it is only Whitehead's "propositions" (or "impure possibilities") which Hartshorne believes to have emerged in time. But this is not the case. For he speaks of "emergent universals other than those which obviously involve particulars, such as 'different from Shakespeare,'" and for examples he cites colors (Whitehead's favorite example of eternal objects).[17] He does hold that among the eternal genera there must be the genus "specificity"; and there must be some set of ultimate variables which serve as the measure of quality. But there need not be any specific qualities that are eternal. Only the absolutely general should be regarded as eternal; the less general is contingent and hence emergent.[18]

Hartshorne further holds that once these universals have emerged, they are still, qua universals, not fully determinate or definite. The name of a particular color refers to a somewhat vague determinable, a similarity between qualities of things, not to an absolutely self-identical quality of a number of different objects. In fact, Hartshorne believes that no two objects or experiences can be said to have precisely the same qualities.[19] "Something like this blue can occur over and over, but not precisely *this* blue." Only the quality qua actualized is fully determinate, and as such it is unique. "Particular qualities in their absolute definiteness are irreducibly relational and historical" (CSPM 64).[20]

latter only to actual entities." "'Determination' is analysable into 'definiteness' and 'position,' where 'definiteness' is the illustration of select eternal objects, and 'position' is relative status in a nexus of actual entities" (PR 38).

[14] "Whitehead's Idea of God," pp. 556f (WP 95); "Interrogation of Charles Hartshorne," p. 329; CSPM 66, 122f, 128.

[15] Hartshorne is referring to PR 340: "But definition is the soul of actuality: the attainment of a peculiar definiteness is the final cause which animates a particular process . . ."

[16] CSPM 62, 65; "Tillich's Doctrine of God," p. 193 in *The Theology of Paul Tillich*, ed. C. W. Kegley and R. W. Bretall (New York: Macmillan, 1952).

[17] CSPM 58f, 63; *Man's Vision of God*, p. 245 (hereafter, MVG).

[18] "Whitehead's Idea of God," pp. 556-58 (WP 95f).

[19] "On Some Criticisms of Whitehead's Philosophy," *The Philosophical Review* 44/4 (July, 1935), 337 (WP 33); CSPM 60, 63; MVG 236.

[20] Hartshorne tries to buttress his position with the claim that "absolute qualitative sameness has no empirical meaning," since the "inability to detect a difference is not the same as ability to detect absolute similarity" (CSPM 64). However, since he normally includes

One way to illustrate the difference between the two philosophers on the nature of qualitative potentiality (even after it has emerged, for Hartshorne), is in terms of the implications for God's knowledge of the future. Whitehead would presumably say that God knows precisely what options are open to a person in the next moment; he only cannot know exactly which set of real possibilities the person will in fact actualize. Hartshorne would say that the exact qualities which the person actualized were not knowable in advance by God even as possibilities. "But that he can do just *this* which he subsequently does, not even deity can know until it is done." This does not impugn the perfection of God's knowledge, for "the 'this' of an actuality simply has no advance status" (CSPM 65). In other words, Whitehead would say God could not know which eternal objects the occasion would select. Hartshorne says the occasion does not merely "select" from fully determinate potentialities, but that it renders the determinable determinate. "There is no such thing as a possible particular. Not even God can fully define a world without creating it" (CSPM 122). Whitehead would say that if an essence is actualized, it must have been antecedently possible; Hartshorne agrees that the possibility must exist prior to the actualization, but insists that it need not be as definite as the quality that actualizes it.[21]

In summary: Hartshorne holds the one eternal object to be the divine essence—the categorical universals with God as envisaging and always somehow applying them. This divine essence, in embodying and constituting the ultimate dimensions or variables, constitutes pure possibility as a continuum of possible states of divine experience.[22] Out of this continuum of possibility emerge qualities which are only relatively indeterminate and time-independent universals. The only wholly determinate qualities are those which emerge in actualities. "Each moment of time will add a little to the definiteness of qualities, even as envisaged by deity."[23]

Hartshorne believes this view has several advantages. First, it would remove a major basis for opposition to the Whiteheadian philosophy by adjusting it to the elements of truth in nominalism, *viz.,* that qualities can be universals without being eternal, that similarity is as ultimate as identity, and that there is no valid basis for affirming eternal specific qualities that are identical in various concrete entities.[24] Second, a "somewhat more

divine experience among the conceivable experiences that could in principle falsify an assertion and hence ground its empirical meaning (CSPM 19, 20f, 171), the statement that two objects embody exactly the same quality would seem to have empirical meaning. Hence, Hartshorne's appeal to God in this regard—"I assume that God knows all non-abstract or wholly determinate qualities of particulars to be unrepeatable" (CSPM 64)—seems to be question-begging. For Whitehead could equally well say that he assumes God to know that different actualities do sometimes embody exactly the same qualities.

[21] "On Some Criticisms of Whitehead's Philosophy," p. 335 (WP 32).
[22] "Interrogation of Charles Hartshorne," pp. 347, 353; MVG 244.
[23] "Whitehead's Idea of God," p. 557 (WP 96).
[24] CSPM 59f, 67; "From Colonial Beginnings," p. 328; "Metaphysics for Positivists," *Philosophy of Science* 2/3 (July, 1935), 294.

nominalistic" view would make Whitehead's type of thought more coherent. The doctrine of eternal objects is a needless complication of the
philosophy of process, and even compromises the ultimacy of creative
process.[25] It makes the process seem to be not genuinely creative, but to
involve only a shuffling of eternal realities, making the temporal world a
mere duplicate reality.[26] The process does not add anything but a vacuous
something called "actuality." In Hartshorne's view, "actualization would
really add something, namely, definiteness."[27]

The preceding comments perhaps point to a further difference. Whitehead held the distinction between possibility and actuality to be absolute
and expressible in terms of value: all actuality has intrinsic value, all possibility is devoid of intrinsic value. Hence Whitehead would say that actualization does add something, namely, value.[28] Hartshorne evidently does
not think of value as being lodged in actuality by virtue of its actuality, but
by virtue of its being wholly definite. For Whitehead, actualization involves
becoming determinate in regard to every item, actual and ideal, in the universe; this determinateness is good in that actuality requires it. For Hartshorne it seems that actuality is good in that determinateness (which he
equates with definiteness) requires it. I suspect this difference lies in part
behind the difference as to whether there are specific qualitative universals.

3. *Secondary Qualities.* The question of this section is whether qualities
as perceived by human subjects by means of their sense organs are to be
predicated of the low-grade entities constituting the gross objects which
appear to have those qualities. Is the redness of the book-image to be
attributed to the molecules of the actual book? That Hartshorne does not
think so is clearly indicated by his position that colors were not possibilities
until there were animals with sense organs.[29] Whatever qualities are to be
attributed to the molecules of the rocks and the cells of the plants, it is not
"grey" and "green" as experienced by us. Accordingly, if Whitehead held
that the same sensum qualifies the experience of both the perceiver and the
individual actualities of the external object, there would be disagreement.

At one time Hartshorne thought Whitehead's position to be the same as

---

[25] "Whitehead's Novel Intuition," p. 20 (WP 163f); "From Colonial Beginnings," p.
328; CSPM xv; RSP 20.

[26] "On Some Criticisms of Whitehead's Philosophy," p. 335 (WP 32); "Tillich's Doctrine of God," p. 193.

[27] "Whitehead's Idea of God," p. 557 (WP 95); cf. *A Natural Theology for Our Time*,
p. 73 (hereafter, NTT). Since Whitehead distinguishes determinateness from mere definiteness (cf. n. 13), he probably would not feel constrained to adopt the doctrine of the indefi-
niteness of possibility to avoid the charge that his actual entities are nothing but reshuffled
complex eternal objects.

[28] Two terms, "position" (n. 13) and "value," have now been used to distinguish the
determinateness of a Whiteheadian actual entity from mere definiteness. The connection between the two is close, for it is an actual entity's position that determines what instrumental
values it can receive from others, and hence largely determines the intrinsic value it will
enjoy.

[29] "Whitehead in French Perspective," p. 577; MVG 245f; CSPM 59f, 63, 65.

his own. Of course, both philosophers reject an absolute bifurcation, according to which sub-animal entities would have only structural properties, while only animals with sense organs would enjoy qualities of sentience. Since all actualities are sentient, there will be some analogy between the kinds of qualities experienced by molecules, cells, and psyches. The only question is, How much analogy? Hartshorne originally thought Whitehead believed that the quality of a clearly focused feeling "will have only a very distant analogy" with the quality of feelings in an external object. The qualities of feelings "will be specific to the kind of organism having the feeling." The most significant sense in which a book in itself can be regarded as red is that its molecules include "as an unimportant but real part our feelings of the redness of the book."[30]

That this was Hartshorne's own view is shown by a similar discussion in *Beyond Humanism,* evidently written at about the same time as the discussion of Whitehead's position just cited. He stresses that the proximate cause of sensation is the body, and that to put sense qualities in external things would be "to substitute an illogical, systematically confused panpsychism for a rational one." The sensed color that is in the brain and mind reacts back upon the external object, but this action is insignificant. It may be that the molecules in the object "themselves feel something like red" and that this feeling is transmitted to photons and then to nerves; but the element of truth in this notion is probably very minimal, "for every feeler to which a feeling is transmitted adds its own individual emotional tone in this chain, so that the end of the chain may not much resemble the beginning."[31] Hartshorne made this point even more clearly in his earliest book, in which he made a strong distinction between the feelings of molecules and those of cells in the optic-nerve circuit. The difference between red as we see it and red as it is in these nerves is merely the difference

> between the individual units of a complex feeling and the complex as a single over-all quality. The characters of the units and complex will not be the same, but they may none the less possess very real similarity. . . . As for the book, it is probably not, in any comparably pregnant sense, red at all.[32]

Hartshorne later, following a criticism from John Blyth and a conversation with Whitehead, agrees with the former that he was mistaken in attributing this view to the latter. It was already clear, he says, that Whitehead meant to affirm that secondary qualities are in nature, since "secondary qualities" are defined as qualities of sentience, and nature is composed of sentient individuals. But, Hartshorne adds, it is not easy

> to determine whether or not he believes that the very *same* qualities as those we enjoy in a given sense-experience are also enjoyed by the extra-bodily objects stimulating

---

[30] "On Some Criticisms of Whitehead's Philosophy," p. 327 (WP 24).
[31] *Beyond Humanism,* pp. 205, 207, 208 (hereafter, BH).
[32] *The Philosophy and Psychology of Sensation,* pp. 248f (hereafter, PPS).

this experience. The passages quoted by Mr. Blyth make it clear that the "red book," or its molecules, enjoy sensa, for all individuals do; but do they enjoy *red* sensa?[33]

Hartshorne then suggests that there are passages in Whitehead supporting both sides of the issue. He also notes that the decisive one on the positive side rests the case for the conformity of sense-appearance to reality on the belief in cosmic teleology, and says that there is no way in Whitehead's epistemology directly to verify the correspondence between qualities as experienced and qualities in external things, whereas there are biological reasons that can be given to justify our knowledge of structural characteristics (the so-called "primary qualities") of things. Finally, he adds that what *is* knowable are the qualities of the body, and that this suffices for the really important issue, i.e., "whether anything, with its qualities, is directly given to us besides just our own 'states,' or 'ideas,' or 'sensa.' " And on this point he and Whitehead are one.[34]

However, prescinding from the question as to which issue is most vital, there does seem to be a real disagreement. It is true that many passages in Whitehead seem to correspond with Hartshorne's view, i.e., that there is so much modification between the molecules of the book, for example, and our perception of it, that there would be little analogy between the qualities of the two sets of occasions. In being transmitted through the bodily cells, Whitehead says, "the datum acquires sensa enhanced in relevance or even changed in character" (PR 183, cf 358). Also the final percipient occasion (the psyche), in one of its originative phases, objectifies the eternal object in the mode of presentational immediacy, thereby transmuting it into a secondary quality (PR 186). This percipient occasion differentiates vague feeling tone into various types of sensa (PR 182). Through this process of modification some eternal objects not in the original set are elicited into important relevance (PR 183).

However, many other passages seem to say that the high-grade occasions can experience the same sensa as the low-grade occasions. Whitehead says that the simplest grade of actual occasions experience a few sensa, and that the sensa are not "purely mental additions," but participate in nature as much as anything else (PR 174, 496). And the following statement is relevant to Hartshorne's question as to whether the molecules in the book experience *red* sensa:

> In their most primitive form of functioning [which in context clearly means in the lowest types of occasions], a sensum is felt physically with emotional enjoyment of its sheer individual essence. For example, red is felt with emotional enjoyment of its sheer redness. (PR 479)

Whitehead elsewhere says that the main characteristic of sensa is their enormous emotional significance; they have their primary status as quali-

[33] "The Interpretation of Whitehead (Reply to John W. Blyth)," *The Philosophical Review* 48/4 (July, 1939), 415f.
[34] *Ibid.*, pp. 416f.

fications of affective tone. And he illustrates by saying that for low-grade entities "green" is "the qualifying character of an emotion."[35]

Accordingly, Whitehead does seem to affirm that the molecules in a red book enjoy red sensa. But there still remains Hartshorne's question, How is red in *this* sense related to red *as we see it*? Would not red as we see it, as a colored shape qualifying an external region, be a different quality from the one enjoyed by the molecules? If so, then the disagreement would be merely verbal. Perhaps Whitehead simply fails to distinguish terminologically between so-called "tertiary qualities" (value experiences), some basic forms of which all occasions enjoy, and "secondary qualities" (sense-data), which only high-grade occasions inheriting from sense organs have. Perhaps he simply uses the term "red" for two different, albeit related, sensa.

But this does not seem to be the case. Whitehead does not generally speak of new eternal objects coming into play somewhere in the process of perceiving (a few possible exceptions were cited three paragraphs above). Rather, he normally speaks of the same sensum acquiring a *new function*. There is said to be some modification of function as the sensa "pass from occasion to occasion along a route of inheritance up to some final high-grade experience" (PR 479, cf 480). But it is in transmutation, effected by this high-grade experient (the psyche), that a radical change occurs. In sense-*reception*, which all occasions enjoy, the sensa are "unspatialized." This means they are simply felt for what they essentially are, i.e., emotional forms. But in sense-*perception* they are "spatialized." This means that "in some occasion of adequate complexity, the category of transmutation endows them with the new function of characterizing nexūs" (PR 174). That is, the same sensum picks up the new function of qualifying an external region.

> In tracing the origin of presentational immediacy, we find mental operations transmuting the functions of sensa so as to transfer them from being participants in causal prehensions into participants in presentational prehensions. (PR 496)

Transmutation involves the following: what is received from the body is a complex eternal object, involving both a sense-datum and a geometrical pattern (PR 260, 475). In the *reception* (i.e., perception in the mode of causal efficacy) the emotional quality is felt vividly, while the geometrical relations are vague, ill-defined, and hardly relevant. "The feeling is blind and the relevance is vague" (PR 247, 262). But in the transmutation basic to presentational immediacy these geometrical "relationships to regions of the presented locus are lifted into distinct, prominent, relevance." The two modes of perception hence deal with the *same* complex eternal object under *different proportions* of relevance (PR 273, 494). This might seem to be denied by Whitehead's statement that the complex eternal object derived from the efficacy of the body must only be "partially identi-

---

[35] *Adventures of Ideas,* pp. 276, 314 (hereafter, AI).

fied with the eternal object in the final feeling of presentational immediacy." But he makes it clear that it is only the geometrical aspect of the complex eternal object that is merely "highly analogous"; the sense-datum involved is the same (PR 475f).

This explanation of transmutation coheres with Whitehead's statement that appearance (the content of presentational immediacy) is "a generalization and an adaptation of emphasis; but not an importation of qualities and relations without any corresponding exemplification in the reality." This is said in response to his own earlier query: "Now when a region appears as red in sense-perception, the question arises whether red is qualifying in any dominant manner the affective tones of the actualities which in fact make up the region" (AI 315, 378).

This interpretation of what Whitehead means may be controversial (frankly, it surprised me). But actually the notion that he means the redness of our experience to differ only in function from that of molecules seems to be implicit in the description of sensa such as red as eternal objects of the subjective species. For, although such an entity is primarily a qualifier of subjective form it can "function both subjectively and relatively." For example, redness may qualify the subjective forms of all the members of a nexus. A psyche objectifies each of the members by a prehension with an analogous subjective form. Then by transmutation redness becomes a characteristic of the nexus as objectified by the percipient (PR 446f).

In conclusion: the differences between the two men on secondary qualities seem to be both verbal and substantive. In regard to the verbal difference, Whitehead sometimes seems to use "secondary" broadly, to cover what many have distinguished as secondary and tertiary. This is especially the case in *Science and the Modern World*. He speaks there of the necessity to "include the secondary qualities in the common world," and he illustrates with colors, sounds, and smells.[36] And yet it is clear that his basic concern is to insist that the natural world is permeated with value.[37] Accordingly, he is more concerned with "tertiary qualities" than with secondary qualities in a narrow sense. And this becomes clearer in later writings with his rejection of the "sensationalist principle," according to which experience would begin with a bare reception of a sense-datum (secondary quality) devoid of any inherent emotional, valuational response.[38] One of the major implications of this rejection is that low-grade entities without sense-organs can enjoy valuational responses to their environments.

Furthermore, as alluded to earlier, in *Process and Reality* he gives "secondary quality" a more precise meaning: when transmutation occurs, an eternal object mediates between the two modes of perception. This eternal object as having ingression in the mode of presentational immedi-

[36] *Science and the Modern World*, pp. 78-80, 132 (hereafter, SMW).
[37] SMW 138, 152, 154, 238, 278, 281, 293.
[38] PR 239, 246; AI 276, 315f; *Modes of Thought*, pp. 148, 152-54 (hereafter, MT).

acy is a secondary quality (PR 99, 186). This red as a mere presentational intuition (Hartshorne's "red as we see it"), separated in consciousness from emotional response, is a high abstraction (PR 247, 480). Accordingly it is clear that in this stricter sense, secondary qualities are not in all actual occasions. In this regard the two philosophers agree: all occasions have tertiary qualities (subjective forms), while only high-grade occasions have secondary qualities, and these are derivative from the tertiary and therefore not completely different in kind.[39] Of course, on the basis of the secondary qualities there may be a derivative origination of subjective form (i.e., more complex tertiary qualities), but this is not the first element of value-experience to occur in the occasion.[40]

However, once this terminological problem is clarified, disagreement still remains on two points. First, Hartshorne thinks in terms of a bigger gap between the qualities enjoyed by our nerve cells and those enjoyed by molecules in external objects. Second, although Hartshorne sometimes writes as if the difference between the qualities enjoyed by us and those enjoyed by our nerve cells were only a difference due to pooling and projecting, i.e., making distinct the inherent spatiotemporal character,[41] he cannot fully equate this with Whitehead's understanding of transmutation (if I have interpreted the latter correctly). For Hartshorne cannot say that the *same* quality is involved, only in a different function. Otherwise reality would not have had to wait upon sense organs for "green" to emerge as a somewhat determinant possibility; rather, it would have emerged as a possibility with the emergence in actuality of living cells.

It should now be clear that the issue in this section is closely related to the earlier discussion of the eternality of qualitative possibility. Hartshorne cannot agree that the same sensum can be involved in molecules, cells, and psyches, for he does not believe there are any specific qualities that subsist as possibilities. Specific qualities exist only as the qualities of actual things. There is something that the molecules, nerve cells, and the psyche have in common when the person objectifies the book as red (assuming normal circumstances, of course), but this something is an extremely vague determinable, which will be rendered determinate by each of these actualities in its own way.

4. *Metaphysical Principles and Philosophic Method.* Many would probably draw a strong contrast between the two men in regard to philosophic method. For is Hartshorne not a rationalist, describing metaphysical truths as *a priori*, evaluating them only in terms of coherence, and being quite confident of the possibility of finding them? And is Whitehead not more of an empiricist, seeing metaphysics as a "descriptive science," invoking the criterion of adequacy as well as coherence, and being quite modest as to the possibility of reaching metaphysical truths?

---

[39] CSPM 76f, 298, 300; PPS 97, 109.
[40] Cf. Whitehead, MT 149, PR 482f; Hartshorne, CSPM 301f.
[41] PPS 115, 136, 248; CSPM 221.

Such a contrast would be overdrawn. First, Hartshorne has endorsed the notion of metaphysics as a descriptive science.[42] This does not conflict with its also being *a priori*, since *a priori* truths are not ones known with certainty, or prior to experience, but ones that could be derived from *any* experience whatsoever. They are simply ones that contradict no conceivable observation, and hence are necessary principles (CSPM 18, 31). And, as Hartshorne points out, Whitehead himself spoke of "necessity" in this connection.[43] It is true that Whitehead said that the primary method of philosophy is descriptive or imaginative generalization, which is "the utilization of specific notions, applying to a restricted group of facts, for the divination of the generic notions which apply to all facts" (PR 8, 15f). But Hartshorne likewise says metaphysics has an inductive aspect: one begins with samples taken from perception and imagination, and then by an intellectual experiment infers that all imaginable entities have such and such properties in common.[44]

In the second place, Whitehead's *Process and Reality* is cosmology as well as metaphysics, and thereby deals with contingencies. Hence it is appropriate even from Hartshorne's point of view that the empirical as well as the rationalistic criteria are invoked, for Hartshorne says that the "coherence theory" of truth is sound only for necessary or metaphysical ideas.[45] Furthermore, he does not reject testing even metaphysical categories for their adequacy (CSPM 19, 39).

Thirdly, Hartshorne has made statements, recently at least, that can match Whitehead's more well-known ones[46] for modesty: metaphysics is "that part of *a priori* knowledge in which clarity and certainty are not readily attained. . . . If what a man most wants is certainty he might better turn his attention to arithmetic, elementary logic, or even some parts of natural science, than to metaphysics" (CSPM 32).[47]

Hartshorne himself has said that Whitehead was close to the sound philosophic method, and that a reasonable view could be worked out in general harmony with his thought on the subject.[48] However, these comments imply some reservation. And he has even spoken of "certain very real methodological deficiencies in Whitehead's metaphysics as now presented," and offers as an example the impossibility of validly grounding the theory of eternal objects.[49] But he elsewhere says that Whitehead's

[42] "On Some Criticisms of Whitehead's Philosophy," p. 341 (WP 36f).

[43] "Whitehead and Contemporary Philosophy," p. 35 (WP 153); cf. PR 5.

[44] "Metaphysics for Positivists," p. 292; CSPM 33.

[45] "Metaphysics for Positivists," p. 290.

[46] E.g., PR x, 294, 300f.

[47] For a further defense of Hartshorne's method as a natural extension of Whitehead's approach, see William M. O'Meara's essay in this monograph.

[48] "Whitehead, the Anglo-American Philosopher-Scientist," *Proceedings of the American Catholic Philosophical Association*, vol. 35 (Washington: The Catholic University of America, 1961), p. 171 (WP 139); "Whitehead and Contemporary Philosophy," p. 35 (WP 153).

[49] "Metaphysics for Positivists," p. 303.

system as such is not strongly committed to the doctrine of eternal objects;[50] so this would not seem to be a serious methodological problem. A statement that might point us in the intended direction is the following:

> Concerning the method and logical status of speculative philosophy: are its statements analytic, synthetic *a priori*, consequences of meaning postulates, phenomenological insights, or what? I find neither Peirce nor Whitehead sufficiently clear at this point, though not so unclear as many of their critics suppose.[51]

Lewis Ford has suggested the following contrast: Hartshorne thinks of metaphysical truths as *analytic a priori*, i.e., their denial is meaningless and their contraries are all self-contradictory. Whitehead's metaphysical truths are *synthetic a priori*, i.e., although they are necessary in the sense of being exemplified in all possible actual entities, they do have non-self-contradictory alternatives. Accordingly, Whitehead's method would be more empirical, Hartshorne's more rationalistic.

Ford's contrast depends upon the following understanding of God's relation to the metaphysical principles: Whitehead thinks in terms of a "primordial decision" which *constitutes* the metaphysical principles. Hartshorne identifies the metaphysical principles with God's eternal nature, and equates the eternal and the necessary. Hence the metaphysical principles are beyond all decision, even God's.

Ford's interpretation is clearly correct in regard to Hartshorne, and it coheres with many of Whitehead's statements, such as the assertion that the primordial realization of eternal objects "at once exemplifies and establishes the categoreal conditions."[52] But Whitehead also says on the same page that God's primordial nature *presupposes* "the *general* metaphysical character of creative advance." But it is precisely this general metaphysical character of creative advance that Hartshorne identifies as the eternal, necessary essence of God.[53] In other words, Whitehead seems to agree that there is a general metaphysical character to reality that is beyond all decision and hence is necessary, without conceivable alternative. Accordingly, at least some metaphysical truths would be "analytic *a priori*," as defined by Ford.

In conclusion I will tentatively suggest the following twofold difference between the two philosophers: First, Hartshorne has thought out much more thoroughly what he means by "metaphysical" truths, and hence what method is needed to reach them. Second, Whitehead seems to distinguish two sets of "metaphysical" categories, i.e., the "category of the ultimate,"[54] and the categoreal principles established by God's primor-

---

dial realization of possibilities. Knowledge of the former would be analytic, knowledge of the latter would be synthetic *a priori*. Hence, while the two men cannot be simply contrasted as rationalist and empiricist, there is for Whitehead an aspect of metaphysical truth that cannot be discovered simply by rigorous reflection upon meanings.

II The Nature of Actuality

5. *Prehensions of Contemporaries.* Hartshorne once held, until about 1960, that Whitehead's system required that contemporary occasions be internally related. His arguments for the possibility and necessity of this were the following:

(1) Internal relations between contemporaries would not destroy their individuality, since each occasion would still reflect the others from its own unique perspective.[55]

(2) Whitehead's doctrine of God as a single actual entity requires internality among contemporaries, since all events prehend God, and he "in his contemporary or consequent nature prehends all actual things."[56]

(3) The previous point holds even if God is conceived as a living person. Since he is not spatially localized, and therefore not spatially separated from anything, there is no transmission with the mere velocity of light between divine and finite events. Hence "it seems no definite lapse of time can occur either between his prehensions of them or theirs of him." Accordingly, since contemporaries "are all immanent in God, and he in turn immanent in them, must they not be immanent in each other?" Furthermore, since Hartshorne at that time thought of the God-world relation as analogous to the mind-brain relation, he suggested that the relation of human consciousness to brain-cell events might be similar.[57]

"one," and which is "presupposed in all the more special categories" (PR 31), to be what is referred to above as the "general metaphysical character of creative advance" (PR 522).

[55] "On Some Criticisms of Whitehead's Philosophy," p. 334 (WP 31); "The Interpretation of Whitehead (Reply to John W. Blyth)," pp. 422f. Because my discussion of contemporaries was itself contemporary with Frederic Fost's essay in this monograph, neither was internally related to the other, and this resulted in some overlap. However, I decided to change my discussion very little in the light of his essay, since our purposes and viewpoints significantly differ. Whereas I am basically cataloguing, Fost is primarily arguing a thesis, and therefore mentions only those issues deemed necessary for his thesis. Also I think Hartshorne's reversal in regard to contemporary relations requires mainly verbal reformulations of his earlier positions. I have accordingly mentioned the ones he has already made, and some further ones he needs. Fost believes this reversal strikes at the heart of some of Hartshorne's commitments. I point out my disagreements with Fost's thesis in fns. 64, 65, 68, and 69.

[56] "On Some Criticisms," p. 334 (WP 31).

[57] "Whitehead's Idea of God," p. 545 (WP 87).

(4) If two contemporary concrete entities are mutually external, then there is the type of vicious regress pointed out by Bradley, for the relations belong to neither of the entities nor to any more inclusive entity.

(5) If the relations between all present contemporaries were all external, the world would not be a real whole.[58] This would endanger the notion of God as the "perfect" or "supreme" being. Against traditionalists who held the world to be external to God's being, Hartshorne countered that then the world-plus-God would be a greater reality than simply God, and therefore God would not be the supreme being, but merely a part of a greater (in value) whole. But this argument, taken strictly, would also count against Hartshorne's own dipolar view of God as living person, *if* God could not prehend contemporaries. Of course, Hartshorne did not hold that God's perfection required that he include future events, since that is impossible, but only that he "have adequate knowledge of events when and as they occur."[59]

However, Hartshorne has explicitly given up all of these views (the second point, of course, was not an argument he used for his own position):

(1) Even before he gave up the idea of internal relations between contemporaries, he apparently began to suspect that such relations would destroy their individuality. In *The Divine Relativity* he says that if there is action one way, there must be action both ways: S^1 would know S^2, and S^2 would know S^1 as knowing it; hence S^1 would know S^2 as knowing itself known by S^1, etc. (DR 99). In later writings he says that "the perceived entity does not perceive its perceiver" (CSPM 217), and clearly rejects the notion that a part depends at all upon precisely that whole of which it is a part, and indicates that this notion of "organic wholes" would lead to absolute idealism. If concrete terms are internal to each other, then "no term can really be distinguished from another; for each includes the other and, by the same logic, the entirety of reality."[60] Two interacting enduring individuals keep their distinctness by virtue of successive states, none of which is influenced by a state of the other individual that it has influenced (CSPM 215). In other words, Hartshorne has apparently come to agree with William A. Christian's statement that "there must be a duration in which the concrescence is closed to further contributions of other data from other individual actual entities," if the occasion is to have subjective unity.[61]

---

[58] "On Some Criticisms," p. 334 (WP 31).

[59] *The Divine Relativity,* pp. 19, 20, 61 (hereafter, DR).

[60] CSPM 212; cf. 83, 103f, 128, 197; LP 199f.

[61] *An Interpretation of Whitehead's Metaphysics* (New Haven: Yale University Press, 1959) p. 60; cf. pp. 330f.

(3) Hartshorne now says that "the factual scientific evidence that time elapses before we see states of affairs is not the essential reason for denying the temporal symmetry of the relation. . . . Perception never should have been taken as simultaneous with its object" (CSPM 217). Here again he has come to agree with Christian, who had said "the fact that light has a uniform, finite velocity is not the categoreal reason for causal independence of contemporaries," so that the lack of spatial separation between God and finite events is no basis for affirming mutual immanence.[62] Hartshorne now holds with Whitehead that, until an entity has become, "there is no definite entity to prehend" so that "experiencing is *never* simultaneous with its concrete objects but always subsequent" (CSPM 109).

(4) Hartshorne now holds that the coexistence of two contemporaries in one space is rendered meaningful by their common pasts and futures. The latter seems the more important—the relation will exist in "any event occurring sufficiently long after two events to have both in its past. . . . They will be coexistent items of *its* past." He does add that, since deity is not localized spatially, at least in the same sense, this picture must somehow be altered or completed by the theistic account, but as to just *how* he cannot understand.[63] But the important point is that, however the picture might be altered, it would no longer be in terms of his earlier position that contemporary entities are contained within the contemporary divine experience as abstractions. Even if God is conceived as a single strand of occasions of experience, each one of which defines a cosmic now, the objectified data of that experience would be the immediately preceding state of the cosmos (CSPM 101).[64]

(5) Hartshorne no longer holds that it is necessary to God's perfection that he include the contemporary as well as past reality of the world. He now denies "interaction between God, as in a certain state, and any other individual in a strictly simultaneous state" (CSPM 115). Since prehensions of contemporaries are now held to be impossible in principle, God's failure to know the contemporary world does not detract from his perfection.[65] In regard to conceiving God as the

---

[62] *Ibid.*, p. 331.

[63] CSPM 219f, cf. 115, 215.

[64] Fost believes the doctrine of the mutual immanence of contemporaries to be correlative with that of a cosmic (divine) simultaneity, such that the denial of the former entails the rejection of the latter. I cannot see that he shows this, or that it is so. Although there are difficulties with the notion of a cosmic simultaneity from the divine perspective, they do not seem to be increased by the denial of God's knowledge of contemporaries. Nor was the affirmation of God's inclusion of all reality Hartshorne's only motivation for affirming a cosmic simultaneity from the divine perspective.

[65] Fost either missed Hartshorne's point here or else disagrees with it. His own sug-

supreme or all-inclusive reality, Hartshorne has said (in conversation) that it is enough if each state of the world is necessarily destined to be included in God.[66] In line with this change of view there is a change in Hartshorne's terminology for occasions of experience. He previously followed Whitehead in speaking of both past and present occasions as *actual* entities.[67] But now he speaks only of past occasions as actual; present ones are said to be only *nascent*. "Presentness is becoming actual rather than being actual" (CSPM 109, 118). This seems motivated in part by the desire to avoid saying that anything actual is unperceived by, and hence outside of, God. Therefore Hartshorne can still define actuality in terms of ideal knowledge, saying that "actual being is what God does perceive" (CSPM 151).[68]

Accordingly, whereas Hartshorne had for many years, against Whitehead's position, affirmed simultaneous interaction, he later came to reject this idea, as he explicitly affirms (CSPM 115, 220; WP 3). However, since this doctrine was so important to him, and he had held it so long, it would not be too surprising if remnants of it appeared in his later statements.

Some of Hartshorne's statements about God are reminiscent of his earlier position that God was the co-subject of every finite subject in its process of becoming. Of course, he explicitly rejects this view now, and speaks of "the everlasting class of 'latest subjects' that have not been objectified" (CSPM 110, cf 115). And yet he affirms with Royce that "all reality" need not be defined independently, but that one can say " 'everything' is simply the entire content of eminent knowledge" (CSPM 288, cf LP 100). But surely that which is "nascent" has reality, albeit not actuality, so that this definition of "all reality" is not quite accurate. Also Hartshorne says we should not speak of "God and the world but the world in God" (CSPM 119, cf LP 105). But if there is always a class of "latest subjects" that have not been objectified, "God and the world" does have a different referent than "the world in God."[69]

gestion that Hartshorne could still ascribe perfection to God as the greatest actual being misses Hartshorne's definition of perfection as the "greatest conceivable."

[66] Cf. CSPM 110; "Whitehead, the Anglo-American Philosopher-Scientist," p. 171 (WP 139).

[67] E.g., "Whitehead's Idea of God," p. 546 (WP 87).

[68] Hence Fost is only partly correct in saying that Hartshorne must give up his idealistic axiom that to be is to be known by God. Hartshorne can no longer say that ideal knowledge defines "reality," but he can say that it defines "actuality." And if he wants to contrast "being" (i.e., actuality) and "becoming," he can still say that "to be is to be known by God."

[69] Fost contends this admission of a contemporary world independent of the present divine actuality vitiates Hartshorne's thesis that the divine essence is the all-pervasive factor of reality. This in turn undercuts the ontological argument, since the "strictly necessary" is

6. *Perishing and Objective Immortality.* There are two somewhat distinct issues involved in regard to Hartshorne's interpretation of Whitehead's views on the perishing of actual occasions and their objective immortality. But they are so closely related that it seems best to treat them together. One issue is whether Whitehead meant the general rule that objectification involves elimination or abstraction to apply also to God's prehension of the world. Some passages suggest that he did, such as the statement that God "loses nothing that can be saved" (PR 525). However, Hartshorne holds that these passages only show that Whitehead wavered on the point. Other statements, as well as the system itself, entail that all actualities in their full individuality must be prehended and preserved forever by God. Whitehead is discussing the temporal world when he says that "objectification involves elimination," and he says there is no metaphysical necessity "why this would be the whole story" (PR 517). Hartshorne refers to passages that develop this idea, such as Whitehead's statement that in God's consequent nature "there is no loss, no obstruction," and that the many are one everlastingly, without the qualification of any loss of individual identity or of completeness of unity. Hence our actions "perish and yet live for evermore" (PR 524, 532f). And, most important for Hartshorne, there is Whitehead's statement that "the truth itself is nothing else than how the composite natures of the organic actualities of the world obtain adequate representation" in the consequent nature of God (PR 18f). If there were any elimination or distorting transformation in God, then this statement would not be true. That is, it could not be true that something was left out or changed "if the truth is just what is retained."[70] Finally, Hartshorne asks how God would be the "supreme exemplification" of the category of prehension if the divine prehensions are limited by abstractness (PSG 284).

Hartshorne suggests that the reference to "nothing that can be saved"

defined as that which is implied by each and every possible thing. If God's essence is not pervasive of the contemporary world, then it is not strictly necessary. However, Fost's own argument is vitiated by a failure to distinguish consistently God's abstract essence from his concrete actuality. It is true that some of Hartshorne's earlier writings referred to God's actuality or subjectivity as coextensive with reality, and he needs to rewrite these passages (e.g., LP 38, 43f, 65, 80f, 85, 98, 99f; MVG 285). Some have already been revised (e.g., WP 103). But the divine essence can still pervade the contemporary world even if the finite events are independent of the contemporary divine actuality. God is a personally-ordered society; his immutable essence is the defining characteristic of each divine occasion. Each worldly event is qualified by the defining characteristic of the contemporary divine occasion, but not because it objectifies that contemporary occasion, as Fost seems to suppose to be necessary, but because it has objectified the previous divine occasion, which by definition has exactly the same essence as the present one. Hence, whether or not Hartshorne's ontological argument is valid, it is not invalidated simply by his admission of the independence of contemporary events.

[70] PSG 284; cf. RSP 212; "Whitehead in French Perspective," p. 575; "Whitehead and Berdyaev: Is There Tragedy in God?" *The Journal of Religion* 37/2 (April, 1957), 77f (WP 191).

might mean that, although the whole event is taken in, "some of the desires and purposes for the future which the event contained must, because of incompatibility, be frustrated."[71] Statements that suggest that the actualities are somehow "transformed" in God might mean "that the data perceived are not altered but that an emergent synthesis is effected which as a whole or unity is more than the world taken collectively and, in this sense only, is a transformation of the world" (PSG 284).

However, even if it is held that there is no abstraction involved in divine prehensions, there are two interpretations of what that might mean. One could hold that, although God's prehension of the finite entity does not abstract from any of *its* prehensions, the finite entity is nevertheless in God only *objectively,* not in its subjective immediacy. That is, although it is not a metaphysical necessity that there be negative prehensions, it is not metaphysically possible for one actuality in its subjective immediacy to be present in another. This is William Christian's interpretation of Whitehead. Or one could hold that the finite entities retain their subjective immediacy in their objective immortality in God. This is Hartshorne's view, and what he believes Whitehead probably meant.

The different interpretations here are not based on the question as to whether Whitehead held God's prehensions to be exceptional; both interpreters agree that he did. The issue really revolves around the interpretation of the "perishing" of finite entities. Since Whitehead said that God inherits from the world "according to the same principle as in the temporal world the future inherits from the past" (PR 531f), the issue is how to interpret the relation between perishing and inheriting in general.

Christian holds to those statements of Whitehead which say that the actual entity perishes when it is complete, and that in perishing the actual entity acquires objectivity and loses subjective immediacy.[72] He cites Whitehead's references to the datum of experience as "dry bones," "secondhandedness," and that which is "divested of its own living immediacy," and his comment that "relatedness is wholly concerned with the appropriation of the dead by the living."[73] Christian holds that Whitehead means that the entity must perish in regard to its subjective immediacy before it can be objectified by another.

Hartshorne knows of these passages, of course, but believes Whitehead's term "perishing" to have been an unfortunate, even dangerous, metaphor.[74] This is partly due to the tendency of some interpreters to take

---

[71] "Whitehead and Berdyaev," p. 77 (WP 191).

[72] PR 44, 126, 130; cf. Christian, *An Interpretation of Whitehead's Metaphysics,* p. 67.

[73] PR ix, 131, 235; cf. Christian, *An Interpretation of Whitehead's Metaphysics,* pp. 65f. Although Hartshorne dislikes speaking of past occasions as "dead," he himself has done so: "But only the dead or the abstract are mere objects." The context makes clear he is speaking of past actual occasions, for he says "only the dead or abstract can be (henceforth) absolute, immune to further influence" (CSPM 120).

[74] "Whitehead's Novel Intuition," p. 22 (WP 165); CSPM 16; "Whitehead on Process: A Reply to Professor Eslick," *Philosophy and Phenomenological Research* 18/4 (June, 1958), 516f; WP 2.

the term so literally as to conclude that the perished entity is no longer actual, and hence cannot be an efficient cause.[75] However, even leaving that extreme interpretation aside, Hartshorne considers the term misleading. For it suggests becoming lifeless, whereas the final word of *Process and Reality* is that occasions "perish, yet live forevermore," to which Hartshorne says he will hold, whether Whitehead always did or not. Also, Whitehead says that occasions "do not change;" but "perishing" connotes a diminution of life, a "drying up of subjective immediacy," and this would certainly be a change.[76] Hartshorne also uses the argument based on Whitehead's equation of truth and the consequent nature of God: if the subjectivity is not contained in God, how can it be true that it occurred?[77]

Accordingly, Hartshorne does not allow that the actual occasion loses subjectivity before it is objectified. Rather, the loss of immediacy in this world is due *solely* to the limits of finite prehenders, that they must abstract from things so much, and hence are not conscious of their immediacy.[78] In line with this view, Hartshorne does not accept the idea that an occasion is *first* past and *then* objectified. "Past" is a relative term, and hence cannot describe a quality of an actual entity in itself; rather, it means that some new present has the entity as its past.[79] "Objectivity is . . . a relation into which subjectivity, by virtue of further subjectivity, can pass" (CSPM 110). "By 'perishing' Whitehead simply means being inherited."[80]

On this interpretation, then, the loss of subjective immediacy involved in ordinary objectification is not due *at all* to some change in the status of the objectified entity, but is due solely to the finitude of the prehenders. Since negative prehension is not a categoreal condition, and is not involved in God's objectification of the world (as Christian agrees), then it follows that all actual occasions are prehended and preserved everlastingly by God in their full immediacy.[81]

Both interpreters recognize that there are several passages that can only with difficulty be reconciled with their respective interpretations. But each believes that his own interpretation does more justice to the relevant texts and to the implications of the basic principles of the system.[82] My own judgment is that Christian's view is more plausible. Be-

---

[75] Review of John Blyth, *Whitehead's Theory of Knowledge,* in *Philosophy and Phenomenological Research* 3/3 (March, 1948), 373. Cf. Christian, *An Interpretation of Whitehead's Metaphysics,* p. 321.

[76] "Whitehead in French Perspective," p. 575; "Whitehead's Novel Intuition," p. 22 (WP 166); CSPM 118.

[77] "Whitehead in French Perspective," p. 575; CSPM 118.

[78] "Whitehead in French Perspective," p. 575; "Whitehead's Novel Intuition," p. 22 (WP 166); Review of John Blyth, p. 374.

[79] "Whitehead's Novel Intuition," p. 22 (WP 165f).

[80] Review of Rasvihari Das, *The Philosophy of Whitehead,* in *The Philosophical Review* 48/2 (March, 1939), 231. Cf. "Whitehead on Process," pp. 516f.

[81] Review of John Blyth, p. 374.

[82] Christian, *An Interpretation of Whitehead's Metaphysics,* p. 344.

sides all the arguments that he marshals,[83] it might be relevant to suggest that Whitehead perhaps used the term "immediacy" in two ways. The passages in which he says that subjective immediacy perishes at satisfaction have been mentioned already. When he speaks in Part V of *Process and Reality* of an immediacy that might not necessarily be lost, it is contrasted not with objectivity as such but with abstraction in the sense of the kind of selection that is required when the characters of things are mutually obstructive (PR 517). Hence the implication need be only that God will not abstract from any of the prehensions of finite occasions, not that their immediacy (in the former sense) will be preserved in their objective immortality.

Of course, Hartshorne will probably find this irrelevant, since he has based his case on a rejection of a literal interpretation of those passages which imply that occasions lose their subjective immediacy on attaining satisfaction. But my impression is that his rejection of the more natural interpretation of these passages was based on the desire to bring them into harmony with the apparent affirmations in Part V of the retention by God of the subjective immediacy of objectified occasions. If Whitehead did use "immediacy" in a different sense here, then there would be no basis for rejecting the literal meaning of those earlier passages.

Also, the argument from truth seems fallacious in this application. For all that is necessary for it to be true that finite occasions had their subjectivity is for God to know, in objectifying them, that in themselves they had subjective immediacy.

Finally, Hartshorne's interpretation may be due in part to his former affirmation that God prehended contemporaries. For on that basis he surely would prehend them in their subjective immediacy, so such a prehension would have to be possible.

7. *Genetic Succession: Real or Logical?* The final issue deals not with God's relation to finite actualities, but with actualities as such. Hartshorne does not agree with Whitehead that one should speak of an actual entity as having "earlier" and "later" parts, as having some phases that are "prior" to others. Hartshorne agrees wholeheartedly with Whitehead's view that the temporal process is not an actual continuum, but is constituted by unit events that are not instants, but have a finite duration. They can undergo a conceptual division, for they are the least actual, not the least possible, parts of time.[84]

But Hartshorne holds that this view not only does not entail, but also forbids, the notion of any succession internal to the occasion. To say that an actual entity has duration or a finite temporal spread, does not entail that it has earlier and later phases, but only that while it becomes a number

[83] *Ibid.,* pp. 50-52, 61-72, 339-49.

[84] "Panpsychism," p. 450 in *A History of Philosophical Systems*, ed. Vergilius Ferm (New York: Philosophical Library, 1950); CSPM 122.

of successive contemporary events might occur.[85] The only kind of succession one can speak of is that between occasions. Whitehead's affirmation of another kind, genetic succession within the occasion, Hartshorne holds to be a mistake. The actual entity does not first have physical prehensions and then mental ones. "The datum is not *first* grasped, *then* thought about (intellectual prehensions), but is grasped thinkingly (so far as there is thought in the experience) from the outset."[86] Any priority involved is only logical, not temporal or some *sui generis* type of priority. And Hartshorne suggests that what Whitehead ascribes to a single occasion is really effected by a short sequence of them. "If there is a succession of acts, first of grasping and then of thinking about, the second act is located in a subsequent actual experience."[87]

NOTE

Some terminological differences also deserve mention. All involve expressions which Hartshorne thinks demean the status of God unnecessarily. He considers the term "principle of limitation (or concretion)" misleading, for Whitehead's God is not merely an abstract principle. When Whitehead first introduced this phrase, with which his view of God has unfortunately been associated, "he perhaps had not yet achieved clarity as to the panentheistic structure of his theism."[88] Whitehead also said that God is "in the grip of" creativity. But the fact that God must always create does not mean he is under the constraint of some external power, any more than his "necessary existence" is a constraint. Just as he could not wish not to exist, "God could not wish not to go on experiencing novel content, since his ideals are incapable of final exhaustive realization. This inexhaustibility of the ideal is again no alien power over God but the intrinsic nature of his own primordial essence" (PSG 271).

Hartshorne grants that one probably cannot reconcile all of Whitehead's statements about creativity, and that some of them suggest that it is a causal factor beyond God. But Hartshorne maintains that creativity should not be thus understood, but should be regarded as the ultimate analogical universal, the common generic abstraction, the form of forms. Whitehead does sometimes thus identify it, and he specifically says it is not an actuality. Hence it cannot be an agent above or alongside God, but only agency as such.[89] Those who point out that Whitehead called it a

[85] "Interrogation of Charles Hartshorne," p. 328; "Whitehead in French Perspective," p. 576; CSPM 114; WP 2.

[86] "Whitehead and Ordinary Language," p. 442 (WP 178f).

[87] "Whitehead in French Perspective," p. 576.

[88] PSG 273; "Whitehead's Idea of God," p. 550 (WP 90f).

[89] "Whitehead's Metaphysics," p. 40 (WP 18f); PSG 276; "Whitehead's Idea of God," p. 526 (WP 72); "Whitehead in French Perspective," p. 578.

"substance" are taking advantage of a passing thought in an early writing (SMW) in which his terminology was not stabilized.[90] Likewise, Whitehead's reference to God as creativity's "primordial creature" involves "indulging in somewhat paradoxical language." Each consequent state of God is a creation, of course; but since there is no first state the divine existence is not something created, and hence is not contingent.[91]

Furthermore, Whitehead could have well emphasized more some aspects of his doctrine of God as creator. "God must, in the system, be eminently creative, and *the* Creator in the only sense which has meaning for Whitehead (and for me)."[92] Also, Whitehead's objection to paying "metaphysical compliments" to God does not mean God is not the greatest conceivable being; the meaning would have been better expressed by saying that one should not try to praise God by talking nonsense about him.[93]

Finally, although Whitehead did not say God is "Creativity Itself" (probably to avoid suggesting that the creatures do not have their own creativity), he could have. First, the distinction between God and creativity is not final, for "all actual creativity is either God's own creative synthesis, or it is a datum for his creative-synthetic action." (Hartshorne should now say, "or it is or will be a datum.") Second, the strictly highest reality exhibits the universal principles in their full meaning, "and in this sense is coincident with that meaning." In his eternal aspects God is no mere case under the categories, for the divine creative process is necessary, and God "is the categories in their pure or unqualified meaning, as fixed characteristics of an individual life within which there is a duality of perfect and imperfect cases, the former always including the latter."[94]

[90] "Whitehead on Process," pp. 517f.
[91] *Ibid.*, p. 519.
[92] "Whitehead in French Perspective," p. 578.
[93] "Whitehead's Idea of God," p. 524 (WP 70).
[94] "Whitehead, the Anglo-American Philosopher-Scientist," p. 171 (WP 134); cf. PSG 276.

CHAPTER IV

Whitehead's Differences From Hartshorne

Lewis S. Ford

In the previous article, David Griffin has expertly and comprehensively catalogued the significant differences between Whitehead and Hartshorne, primarily as these appear from a Hartshornian perspective. I think the differences take on a somewhat different shape from a Whiteheadian point of view, particularly with respect to possibility. Moreover, I hope to show that most of these particular differences can be traced to a single root cause: Hartshorne is more resolutely and single-mindedly temporalistic in outlook. Both wholeheartedly subscribe to the dictum that "apart from the things that are actual, there is nothing—nothing either in fact or in efficacy,"[1] but this is understood by Hartshorne to refer solely to "things that are *temporally* actual.*" Whitehead, however, considers God to be a nontemporal actuality and places great weight on his primordial, nontemporal envisagement. First, I wish to consider the issue of eternal possibilities in some detail, then take up more briefly the other differences noted by Griffin in seriatim to show to what extent they depend upon this temporalistic restriction. Finally, I shall consider some additional differences, primarily arising out of the denial of eternal objects, that become more evident from a Whiteheadian perspective.

I. The Nature of Eternal Possibilities

Hartshorne persuasively argues (a) "that all specific qualities, i.e., those of which there can be negative instances in experience, are emergent," (b) that these are emergent from an infinite affective continuum without definite parts, and (c) "that only the metaphysical universals are eternal."[2] These theses are put forward in explicit opposition to Whitehead: "I do not believe that a determinate colour is something haunting reality from all eternity, as it were, begging for instantiation, nor that God primordially envisages a complete set of such qualities. At this point I am no Whiteheadian" (CSPM 59). I do not wish to challenge these theses, which properly qualified I hold to be correct, but I do question the interpretation of Whitehead which puts him at odds with them.

[1] *Process and Reality*, p. 64. Hereafter, PR.
[2] *Creative Synthesis and Philosophic Method*, pp. 59, 66. Hereafter, CSPM.

WHITEHEAD'S DIFFERENCES FROM HARTSHORNE 59

Serious ambiguity surrounds such words as the "eternal" or "eternity." They contrast with the "temporal," that which is instanced at some time or other, but they can refer either to that which is atemporal (independent or divorced from time), or to that which is everlasting (always instantiated in time). Whitehead initially understood the eternal in this second sense and rejected it as a suitable designation for his "objects." In a letter to Norman Kemp Smith dated January 24, 1924 he wrote: "the main point in your lecture with which I disagreed was the statement that I considered 'objects' (and in particular 'sensa') as 'eternal.' I should not call them 'eternal' because (as stated in my *Principles of Natural Knowledge*) I do not consider them as 'in time' in the primary sense of the phrase. I should call an unending event eternal."[3] Yet barely a year later Whitehead introduced the term "eternal object" in *Science and the Modern World*, without significantly altering his view on the relation of formal characteristics to temporal events. Rather, he chose now to interpret "eternal" as "atemporal" rather than as "everlasting": "A colour is eternal. It haunts time like a spirit. It comes and it goes. But where it comes, it is the same colour. It neither survives nor does it live. It appears when it is wanted."[4] This is well understood with respect to actual occasions. Yet while only sporadically ingredient in temporal actuality, eternal objects are often assumed to be permanent possibilities, everlastingly "subsisting," because envisaged by God "from all eternity," i.e., from time immemorial. Eternal objects endure as possibilities throughout all time, it is claimed, because God is always conceptually prehending them.

I think it would be more accurate to say that God *never* (at no time) prehends all the eternal objects. There is no one particular time or other when he prehends all of them. To be sure, the *primordial* envisagement is complete, including all eternal objects (PR 46, 47, 70, 134), but that act is precisely nontemporal, not occurring in time. As primordial, God "is not *before* all creation, but *with* all creation" (PR 521). This means not only that there never was a time in which God sat enthroned in solitary splendour "before the creation of the world," but that the primordial nature itself is temporally emergent *with* creation, emerging when relevant and as needed. Such nontemporality is difficult to conceive, because we are so time-bound. To be sure, "every actual entity is . . . 'out of time' so far as its mental pole is concerned" (PR 380), but all our pure conceptual prehensions—and those of all other actual occasions—take place at definite times, because the subjects of those prehensions are limited to particular spatiotemporal locations. This need not be true of God's pure conceptual prehensions of the eternal objects; they need not be at any particular place in space and time. Of course, by the ontological principle, they must be "somewhere," but "This 'somewhere' is the non-temporal actual entity," the primordial mind of God

---

[3] This letter is published in the *Southern Journal of Philosophy* 7/4 (Winter, 1969-70), 339.

[4] *Science and the Modern World*, p. 126.

(PR 73), which does not refer to some particular space-time, let alone to all space-times.

This is precisely the point at which the Hartshornian principle of temporal restriction comes to bear: that which is nowhere in space and time is nonexistent. If the primordial nature is conceived to be existent, it must be conceived to be ingredient in time. We cannot, however, interpret Whitehead as holding the primordial envisagement to take place from time to time, because he insists on its unity, completeness, and all-inclusiveness. Since, however, the consequent nature is everlasting, it may be conceived as including the primordial nature everlastingly within itself as the concrete includes the abstract. Thus Hartshorne speaks of "that which God primordially or at all times is."[5]

The interpretation is even more pronounced if we adopt Hartshorne's emendation and conceive of God as a personally ordered society of occasions. Each divine occasion then inherits the primordial nature from its predecessor as the defining characteristic of that personal society, such that in every moment God re-enacts his complete envisagement of all eternal objects. The implications of this approach for the eternal objects has been most fully worked out by John Cobb.[6] He conceives of the primordial nature as a permanent ordering of the eternal objects in "an indefinite variety of orders. God's ordering of possibilities is such that every possible state of the actual world is already envisioned as possible and every possible development from that actual state of the world is already envisioned and appraised. Thus, the one primordial ordering of eternal objects is relevant to every actuality with perfect specificity."[7] Thus the primordial nature is a crystalline structure of branching alternative possibilities always present to God, who needs only to match the appropriate branching with the actual course of affairs to select the right initial aims for occasions. The programming is already complete beforehand, and needs only to be put to use. Hartshorne's unhappiness with such a model seems all too justified. Why not streamline the primordial nature, jettisoning this permanent structure of possibility as unwanted metaphysical baggage, restricting it simply to that which is required to define the divine society, namely, the abstract divine essence?

[5] "Whitehead's Idea of God," in *The Philosophy of Alfred North Whitehead*: The Library of Living Philosophers, ed. Paul A. Schilpp (Evanston and Chicago: Northwestern University Press, 1941), p. 530, reprinted in *Whitehead's Philosophy: Selected Essays, 1935-1970*, p. 75 (hereafter, WP). Then all the eternal objects, as ingredient in the primordial nature are "common to all possible events, regardless of date" (WP 116), though Whitehead holds only a selection need be felt by any occasion (PR 366).

[6] *A Christian Natural Theology* (Philadelphia: Westminster, 1965), pp. 155f, 196-203.

[7] *Ibid.*, pp. 155f. As Griffin has pointed out to me, Cobb rejects the association of initial aims exclusively with the primordial nature in his own revision of Whitehead's doctrine. The initial aim is here understood as a propositional feeling drawing upon God's consequent experience, a feeling which may also be influenced by the anticipatory feelings of its predecessors. See *ibid.*, pp. 179-83, 189. The passage I have quoted, however, represents his interpretation of the primordial nature's contribution to the initial aims.

But if the primordial nature is nontemporally existent, such moves are unnecessary. Possibilities may be conceived as temporally emergent, but in terms of propositions, not simply in terms of eternal objects. In fact, all of God's conceptual entertainment of eternal objects with respect to time requires propositional feeling. The integration of his pure conceptual feelings of the eternal objects with indicative feelings derived from his consequent nature is the way in which portions of the primordial nature become temporally emergent. Since that nature is infinite and inexhaustible, at no time has it (or will it) become fully emergent in time. Whatever God physically prehends of the actual world, he experiences ever afterward, but he conceptually prehends (in temporal, propositional feeling) only those eternal objects relevant to his physical experience, whether to provide that experience with its conceptual unification or to provide appropriate possibilities for actualization.

Here we need to distinguish between pure and real possibilities. (Such a distinction finally makes no sense on Hartshornian grounds, since all pure possibilities must be ontologically grounded in nontemporal actuality.) Pure possibilities are all those eternal objects capable of constituting (in whole or in part) the "forms of definiteness" for actual occasions. The primordial envisagement entertains all such pure possibilities, but these cannot be construed as including "every possible state of the actual world" as proposed by Cobb.[8] Every state of the actual world, possible or actual, has a particular extensive (spatiotemporal) standpoint, each with its own share of past actualities which are potentials for it. Pure possibilities, in themselves divorced from time, have neither temporal standpoints nor reference to past actualities. Real possibilities have both, for they are propositions whose predicative patterns are the pure possibilities primordially envisaged coupled with logical subjects specifying the past actualities which are the potentials for this actualization. When attached to such logical subjects, the predicative pattern does specify a particular spatiotemporal standpoint (or range of standpoints), namely, those locations at which the indicated past actualities can be unified in a new actualization.

The really possible is dependent upon past actuality. It is possible for me to become President of the United States, but not nearly to the degree to which this is possible for Ted Kennedy or John Connally, while it is no longer a possibility for William Jennings Bryan. In one sense, this requirement is a restriction upon the domain of pure possibility, but more importantly this dependence upon past actuality is precisely what *enables* such selected "forms of definiteness" to characterize actual occasions which may come into being, since every actualization is a unification of the past actualities which are potentials for it. Put another way, the specified pure possibility may designate the formal cause of the projected actuality, but this is incapable of actualization apart from the concomitant material

---

[8] *Ibid.,* p. 155.

cause supplied by the past. Each past actual occasion is individually determinate, but by the fourth category of explanation (PR 33) it is a potential for further determination, since it is contributory to a new many requiring unification (PR 32). Unity is determinate, but multiplicity is indeterminate, even when composed of determinate unities, and thus the past actualities collectively constitute the indeterminate but determinable "matter" to be actualized according to the formal cause. (This is an interesting reversal of Aristotle. The efficient cause effecting or bringing about such actualization cannot be grounded in some past actuality, for it is dead, inert "matter." It is the creativity inherent within each occasion which must be such a "productive" or "moving" cause.)[9]

This general structure applies to all real possibilities, even to those referring to the remote future. Here the past actualities such propositions refer to constitute but a small fragment of the total actual world needed to bring that possibility to fruition. Here it is possible to agree with Hartshorne: "An old query is, 'Which is prior, actuality or possibility?' Actuality is prior in the sense that every case of futurity involves a case of pastness, i.e. of actuality. What is possible next is simply what is compatible with what has happened up to now. Possibility without actual antecedents is merely the abstraction from every definite stage of process" (CSPM 68). Yet this analysis slights what we have called the formal cause with respect to possibility. The possible is not merely compatible with the past out of which it grows, but provides the formal pattern for the emergence of the actual. In this limited sense the possible is prior to the actual, but such possibility is rooted itself in a 'prior' nontemporal actuality.

If all real possibility is dependent upon past actuality, then it is temporally emergent, even for God. If there are also pure possibilities, they are grounded in what is purely nontemporal, and there is no need to assume (apart from the Hartshornian principle of temporal restriction) that these must be entertained by God at some time or other. For it is only as ingredient in real possibilities that pure possibilities are ever relevant to the course of events, a relevance achieved precisely by such propositional feelings. Moreover, propositional feelings are necessary presuppositions for conscious experience according to Whitehead's technical theory of consciousness (PR 406-20), and there is no reason not to apply these requirements to divine consciousness. We tend to assume that the primordial nature is everlasting and conscious, but Whitehead explicitly tells us it is nontemporal and unconscious (PR 524). Consciousness, with its reference to the physical

<hr>

[9] This analogy between the past actual world in its role as potentiality for subsequent concrescence and Aristotelian proximate matter is also developed by Richard Rorty in "Matter and Event," pp. 497-524 in *The Concept of Matter*, ed. Ernan McMullin (Notre Dame: University of Notre Dame Press, 1963), especially pp. 510f, 514f. Rorty also notes (p. 517, n. 35) that "Whitehead himself was inclined to analogize 'primary matter' to 'Creativity' (PR 46)— which, however, he also analogizes to primary substance (PR 32)." Ivor Leclerc develops those analogies in *Whitehead's Metaphysics* (London: George Allen and Unwin, 1958), pp. 81-87.

prehension of actuality, is necessarily temporal, but the divine consciousness can call upon infinite depths of unconscious conceptual feeling for the
imaginative elaboration of whatever experience God temporally en-
counters.

Let us return to our initial three theses, considering them individually.
(a) All specific qualities are temporally emergent. The emergence of specific qualities into actuality is dependent upon the effective use of the category of conceptual reversion, whereby the novel quality is first realized in
temporal actuality. To be sure, Whitehead speaks of this category as having
been abolished (PR 382, cf 377) in the sense that it allows apparent exceptions to Hume's principle of the derivation of conceptual experience from
physical experience. For where has Hume's missing shade of blue come
from? In the complete account, such unrealized eternal objects must be derived from the occasion's hybrid physical prehension of God's graded alternative relevancies for that occasion. This graded valuation both supplies
the unrealized eternal objects and the proximate relevance to the realized
eternal objects derived from the past. Despite its "abolition," the category
of conceptual reversion is retained (e.g., PR 397, 398, 425) in order to em-
phasize that "reversion is always limited by the necessary inclusion of elements identical with elements in feelings of the antecedent phase" (PR
381), i.e., with realized eternal objects derived from past actualities. To
invoke our language of formal and material causation, we may say that an
emergent, specific quality, realized for the first time, has only a partial material cause because the new can only be partly derived from the old, com-
pensated for by a more complete formal cause. Yet even though this formal
possibility is derived from God, ultimately from his primordial envisagement, that possibility is dependent upon the occasion's past actual world,
to which the novel possibility is judged to be relevant by God's propositional
feeling. Thus we may agree with Hartshorne that there may well have been
a time when God did not consciously experience blue,[10] though not because
blue had not yet been realized in the actual world, but because this quality,
nontemporally existent in the primordial unconscious, did not effectively
contrast with the actual world to make its presence temporally and consciously felt.

Now Hartshorne's account of the emergence of particular qualities is
considerably simpler. Since the contrasts universal-particular and possible-
actual are modally coincident, "no possibility is literally particular, no
universal is literally actual" (CSPM 61). As Eugene H. Peters has put it,
the potential is part of the actual.[11] Possibilities are determinables, partially
indefinite universals derived from past actuality awaiting future determination. Such determination renders such indefinite qualities both actual and
fully particular. "The ultimate principle is experiencing as partly free or

[10] *Man's Vision of God*, pp. 245f.
[11] *Hartshorne and Neoclassical Metaphysics* (Lincoln: University of Nebraska Press, 1970), p. 82.

self-creative, and this principle, being ultimate, accounts for definiteness without help from any other principle" (CSPM 62). Thus each act of self-determination may well produce its own specific and particular quality from a more indefinite universal possible quality. "Something very like this blue can occur over and over, but not precisely *this* blue. Particular qualities in their absolute definiteness are irreducibly relational and historical" (CSPM 64). Yet this seems to be in some tension with Hartshorne's acceptance of prehension, which is "a theory of literal identity, the same entities entering over and over again into subsequent entities" (CSPM 60). Apparently Hartshorne holds that what is contained in my experience is identical with what I experience, but that what I actualize may be merely similar to that upon which the actualization is based. But for Whitehead, *how* I experience is *what* I actualize (PR 34f).

Hartshorne's account makes no distinction between "definiteness" and "determinateness," terms carefully distinguished in Whitehead's twentieth category of explanation (PR 38). Determinateness requires not merely the definiteness of eternal objects, but "position" as well, i.e. "relative status in a nexus of actual entities." Such position is more than simply spatiotemporal location, for it signifies that the determinate actuality is emergent from that particular past actual world which is potential for it.[12] Thus determination is not, as on Hartshorne's view, rendering specific and particular a somewhat general and universal possibility. That would entail an illegitimate appeal to the explanatory power of creativity, for something (the concreteness, the particularity) would have floated in from nowhere. The ontological principle, which vests all reasons in actual entities, understands these reasons in terms of the creative activity of decision, "used in the root sense of a 'cutting off' " (PR 68). Hartshorne's occasion is given too little (an indefinite, somewhat universal quality), from which it must produce more (the concrete definiteness). Whitehead's occasion is given too much (the vast multiplicity of past actualities, plus the entire range of relevant alternative possibilities of unification, each completely definite), which it must pare down to size by selecting one of these possibilities by means of which to organize together whatever is compatible from the past actual world. Creativity achieves novel determinateness by unifying past determinate actualities, but not by rendering definite that which was merely indefinite, which entails deriving the more from the less.

Compared with Whitehead's account of possibility, Hartshorne's is more one-dimensional, resting on the determinable-determinate contrast. That which is determinable must be partially indefinite, universal, abstracted from the actual. That which is determinable on Whitehead's account is fully determinate, particular, and actual taken individually, indeterminate only as a multiplicity awaiting further unification. This potentiality of past actu-

---

[12] Griffin notes this point in fn. 13; see also fns. 27 and 28. His comment is well taken that for Whitehead all actuality has intrinsic value, in contrast with possibility, which is devoid of intrinsic (though not of instrumental) value.

ality must be coupled with possibility in the guise of "forms of definiteness" for such unification. Actualization requires the intersection of possibility with potentiality for its fruition. But Hartshorne's theory has no place for definite possibilities.

(b) These specific qualities are emergent from an infinite affective continuum without definite parts. Here qualification is in order in terms of our distinction between definiteness and determinateness. The determinate is separable, while the merely definite is distinguishable but not separable. The continuum of possibility has no determinate parts, for no individual possibility can be separated from its relevant alternatives save as it is actualized. Moreover, insofar as possibilities are temporally entertained in real possibility, they are selected out of a continuous background which cannot be duplicated by any temporal process of juxtaposing possibilities. All temporally emergent possibilities spring from an infinite continuum which is more than these definitely articulated alternatives. None of this, however, precludes there being a qualitative continuum nontemporally constituted by a dense infinity of eternal objects ordered in terms of their individual essences. I take the primordial nature, on one level of its being, to constitute just such a qualitative continuum.

(c) Only the metaphysical universals are everlasting in the sense of always being exemplified in actuality and in always being prehended by God. All other eternal objects are only actualized from time to time in temporal actuality, since they bear no metaphysical necessity, and they are only conceptually entertained in divine temporal propositional feeling when somehow related to contingent temporal actualities. The metaphysical universals form the predicative patterns of those metaphysical propositions (PR 300-303) which apply to all actualities without exception. These propositions are thus everlastingly felt by God, even though the pure possibilities ingredient in them have their ultimate locus in God's nontemporal nature.

II. THE OTHER DIFFERENCES NOTED BY HARTSHORNE

Let us now briefly consider the differences catalogued by Griffin in the light of Hartshorne's rejection of any nontemporal actuality:

1. *The Divine Polarity.* Is God a society of occasions or a single actual entity? Here I think the issue finally turns on whether the notion of a nontemporal unification is intelligible, for this is essential to Whitehead's systematic contrast between God and the World which rests upon the genetic priority of the mental and the physical poles with respect to one another (PR 54).[13]

This contrast is based upon two complementary, contrasting ways in which the many actualities of the temporal world may be unified in concrescence, which we may designate in terms of "perspectival elimination"

[13] This systematic contrast is explored in detail in my essay on "Whitehead's Categoreal Derivation of Divine Existence," *The Monist* 54/3 (July, 1970), 374-400.

and "conceptual supplementation." In physical, spatiotemporal unification, where the physical pole is prior, incompatible aspects of the many occasions of the past actual world are perspectivally eliminated to conform to the specific standpoint of the concrescing occasion. In conceptual unification, on the other hand, such incompatibilities are not eliminated, since everything is positively prehended within an all-inclusive unity, and they are absorbed into a wider harmony of meaning. Such conceptual supplementation is analogous to Whitehead's favorite method of philosophical reconciliation whereby conflicting principles are adjusted to one another by being placed within an over-arching conceptual structure. Or we may appeal to the aesthetic analogy in which clashing sounds or colors are transformed into a harmonious whole by becoming part of a patterned unity which permits them to be integral elements enhancing one another. By such conceptual supplementation, each actuality is allowed to be fully itself in the divine experience, yet contributing to a harmonious unity by virtue of the larger, all-inclusive patterned contrast God draws from the inexhaustible depths of his nontemporal primordial nature.

Such conceptual unification is nontemporal, not restricted to any one space or time by perspectival elimination. If such nontemporal unification is excluded, Whitehead's systematic contrast between God and the World based upon these two contrasting modes of unification collapses, and the distinction between actual entities and actual occasions is lost. Then God does indeed become an exception to the metaphysical principles, which can be remedied only by treating God as a personally ordered society of occasions, thereby assimilating the concept of God as much as possible to the theory of actual occasions, allowing only the mode of spatiotemporal unification. To be sure, God is ordinarily conceived here to be omnispatial, so that no questions of perspectival elimination based on any differences in spatial standpoints between God and the World need arise. Whether there is any perspectival elimination based on differences in temporal standpoints depends on how we interpret the perishing of occasions, to be discussed below. In any case, God is here conceived in terms of an unending series of successive temporal unifications of the world, each perfectly and completely including its immediate predecessor as well as all those new actual occasions which have come into being in the meantime.

Such successive, omnispatial, temporal unifications of the world do constitute Whiteheadian durations, temporal cross-sections of the universe as a whole, thereby designating privileged meanings to simultaneity contrary to relativity physics. Because of this difficulty, Hartshorne has of late toyed with the possibility of conceiving God as a complex society of spatiotemporal divine occasions, all inheriting a common divine essence and interrelated by greatly overlapping pasts and futures, but whose contemporary members would prehend the world in causal independence from one another (CSPM 123-25). Apart from "the faint odor of polytheism" (Paul Fitzgerald's apt description) that surrounds this proposal, it does have strong affinities with my own previous resolution of this problem, as Griffin properly notes.[14] But I now think that approach errs insofar as it treats the mode of divine unification as spatiotemporal rather than nontemporal, for any account of spatiotemporal unification entails perspectival elimination contrary to God's nature. I now hold that God physically prehends each actuality in terms of its own spatiotemporal standpoint, unifying that prehension with his other physical prehensions by means of conceptual supplementation, not in terms of any other spatiotemporal standpoints. As we have seen from our discussion of real possibility, however, God does generate propositional feelings defining new standpoints and actual worlds for nascent occasions, such that a nascent occasion receives from God a conceptual valuation of the actual world available to that particular standpoint, but that is not the same as God's physical feeling relative to that standpoint, which only arises after that nascent occasion has achieved its concrescence. Prior to that achievement, God entertains a real possibility for that standpoint rather than physically prehending the world from that standpoint.

2. *Eternal Possibilities.* This was sufficiently discussed as the topic of our first section.

3. *Secondary Qualities.* Here we are much indebted to Griffin's thorough analysis, showing that while all occasions have tertiary qualities (i.e., subjective forms), only high-grade occasions have secondary qualities derivative from these. Yet while Whitehead explains this in terms of the diverse ways in which the same quality (eternal object) functions, Hartshorne permits an indefinite qualitative possibility to be concretely particularized as a novel specific quality by the high-grade organism. Clearly what is at stake here depends upon their different approaches to the nature of possibility, transposed to the problem of quality. In the name of a generative creativity Hartshorne allows for a more relaxed interpretation of the principle that "ex nihilo nihil fit," while Whitehead can afford to insist upon a strict interpretation in virtue of his infinite nontemporal reservoir of specific qualities. In sense-perception there can be "a generalization and an adaptation of emphasis; but not an importation of qualities and relations without any corresponding exemplification in the [antecedent] reality."[15]

4. *Metaphysical Principles and Philosophic Method.* Griffin correctly indicates the large measure of agreement that exists here: for both metaphysics is descriptive of the generic features of all experience. Nonetheless, there are real differences. Hartshorne holds that metaphysical principles are exemplified in all experience because they have no genuinely conceivable, self-consistent alternatives. Thus much of his philosophical endeavour can follow the rationalistic method, so assiduously followed by Brand Blanshard, of demonstrating the incoherence of all proposed alternatives.

[14] See my essay, "Is Process Theism Compatible with Relativity Theory?" *Journal of Religion* 48/2 (April, 1968), 124-35, especially pp. 131-34, and Paul Fitzgerald, "Relativity Physics and the God of Process Philosophy," *Process Studies* 2/4 (Winter, 1972).

[15] *Adventures of Ideas*, p. 378. Hereafter, AI.

This is nicely brought out in Eugene H. Peters' *Hartshorne and Neoclassical Metaphysics*. Chapter two, "The Methodological Key," develops the principle, while successive chapters uphold panpsychism, creationism, and neoclassical theism by demolishing materialism and dualism, determinism, empirical theism and atheism as inconsistent alternatives. For Whitehead, however, the metaphysical principles are always exemplified in order to give the universe a fundamental stability, and they are established in this role by God. God as the principle of limitation, as I interpret it, means that alternatives to the metaphysical principles may well be self-consistent, though never actualizable. Logic and mathematics explore the nature of self-consistent systems, while metaphysics must look to experience to see which one is generically exemplified. Thus Whitehead's characteristic approach leans heavily on generalization and synthesis, taking theories derived from science, religion, art, culture and common sense, noting their limited contexts of applicability, and reconciling them wherever possible within a wider context of meaning.

This difference hinges on the intelligibility of a divine nontemporal decision. Whitehead writes that "this ideal realization of potentialities in a primordial actual entity constitutes the metaphysical stability whereby the actual process exemplifies general principles of metaphysics" (PR 64), for God's "conceptual actuality at once exemplifies and establishes the categoreal conditions" (PR 522). Decision for Whitehead "constitutes the very meaning of actuality" (PR 68), so it is in virtue of this nontemporal decision that God is a primordial actuality, nontemporally complete, though as such deficient in temporal actuality (PR 521, 524). Hartshorne criticizes Whitehead's talk of God as the "primordial creature" of creativity on the grounds that the divine essence must be uncreated, but for Whitehead the primordial nature is not uncreated but self-created, thereby an instance of creativity. Since every decision is objectively a reason, we look to God "for reasons of the highest absoluteness" (PR 28).

For Hartshorne every decision must be a temporal decision, and it makes no sense to suppose that any temporal decision, no matter how remotely past, could determine the metaphysical principles. Such a decision either initiates the temporal process, thereby contravening the everlastingness of creativity whereby every event grows out of an actual past, or it presupposes a past domain in which the metaphysical principles did not hold sway, contrary to their absolute universality. Moreover, every temporal decision is a limitation upon antecedent possibility, whereas the metaphysical principles determine the boundary between the possible and the impossible. Whatever is in accordance with the metaphysical principles is possible, and may become actual under the appropriate contingent conditions, but whatever is incompatible with them is impossible for all time, since nothing can become actual which does not exemplify them. Any divine temporal determination of the metaphysical principles thus already presupposes them as informing the antecedent possibilities among which he is supposed to choose.

Since no temporal activity could possibly establish the metaphysical principles, Hartshorne must suppose they are uncreated. Yet it cannot simply be arbitrary that these principles are so and not otherwise. Both thinkers subscribe to the ontological principle requiring that all reasons be grounded in the decisions of actual entities, but no such reason can be given for metaphysical principles if the temporalistic restriction is in force. For Hartshorne, however, no reason need be given, simply because these principles admit of no genuine alternatives. The absence of truly conceivable alternatives is necessary to protect metaphysics from ultimate arbitrariness.

Yet metaphysical principles can be created if we permit nontemporal activity accompanying the temporal process, situated neither at the purported beginning of time nor somewhere in its middle. The primordial act is not a decision amid antecedent possibility, for it is the very creation of possibility itself. I interpret the primordial envisagement to be the activity of interrelating the eternal objects as bare individual essences (sheer qualities) by providing each with its specific relational essence, thereby generating a domain of pure possibility. Each of these pure possibilities contains as part of its relational essence the metaphysical principles, for it is in virtue of these principles that that complex eternal object is capable of becoming actual. Not every eternal object, however, is either a pure possibility or a constituent element within a pure possibility. Those eternal objects whose relational essences are incompatible with the metaphysical principles are excluded. The primordial envisagement is a decision in the sense that it determines which eternal objects are capable of actualization and which are not in the process of creating their relational essences. Alternatively, we may say that God nontemporally decides what the metaphysical principles are. [16]

Thus the domain of what is logically conceivable is larger than the domain of what is metaphysically possible. Whatever can be the datum of a pure conceptual prehension, that is, any eternal object, is logically conceivable. Logical inconceivability arises from the failure to integrate into one conceptual prehension the prehensions of two or more eternal objects which are incompatible by reason of their relational essences. Thus there may be sets of mutually consistent eternal objects (i.e. eternal objects whose systematic interrelationships are genuinely conceivable) which are nevertheless forever incapable of actualization, because they are not consistently conceivable together with the metaphysical principles. These alternatives to the metaphysical principles are excluded from actualizability by the primordial decision, though it must be stressed that God does not choose between sets of logically consistent metaphysical alternatives, because that primordial act itself creates both the metaphysical principles and its alternatives as features of the relational essences of the uncreated sensa.

Alternatively, we may think of metaphysical principles as *a priori*

---

[16] This issue is developed in detail in my essay on "The Non-temporality of Whitehead's God," forthcoming in the *International Philosophical Quarterly* (March, 1974).

because they are presupposed by every actualizable experience whatsoever. Whereas Hartshorne considers them to be *analytic a priori* truths because all alternatives are inconsistent, Whitehead regards them to be
synthetic a priori principles. They may well have consistent alternatives, so we must look to experience to see which metaphysical principles
are in fact being exemplified. Yet whatever principles are exemplified,
they must be necessarily exemplified in the sense that every actuality whatsoever, past, present, or future, must exemplify them. Otherwise they are
merely cosmological principles, lacking full metaphysical generality.

Griffin suggests that there must be at least some metaphysical truths
that would be analytically true for Whitehead, since the primordial decision, the basic reason for all synthetic metaphysical principles (PR 28)
"presupposes the *general* metaphysical character of creative advance"
(PR 522). I interpret this character to be very general, simply the creative
activity of unification. God's own self-creative decision presupposes this
creative drive toward unity as its primordial exemplification, but this sheer
creativity acquires whatever character it has from the actual entities which
instantiate it, receiving from God its "primordial character" (PR 522).[17]

Creativity is "that ultimate principle by which the many . . . become
one" (PR 31), but is it a metaphysical principle? Not if all metaphysical
principles are metaphysical propositions whose predicative patterns are
exemplified in each and every actual entity (PR 300-303). Then a principle
has a pattern of eternal objects, while creativity is precisely that which contrasts most radically with eternal objects. Whitehead resorts to language of
principles and categories in describing "The Category of the Ultimate" because he has no other language in which to describe the ultimacy and all-
pervasiveness of this restless, unificatory activity at the heart of his metaphysical vision. Can this be appropriately defined in terms of some metaphysical essence? Can it be expressed in terms of an *a priori* truth, whether
analytic or synthetic?

The closest Whitehead comes to such a truth is the simple statement:
"It lies in the nature of things that the many enter into complex unity"
(PR 31). Since this is a statement, its meaning may be either analytic or
synthetic. While I hold it to be profoundly true, the deepest insight of
Whitehead's philosophy and its organizing intuition,[18] I cannot see that it
is analytically true. There is nothing inconsistent about saying that the
many simply remain many; in fact, this is the overwhelming deliverance of
common experience, superficially analyzed.

No reason can be given for creativity, for it cannot be explained either

[17] The application of creativity to God's primordial decision poses some problems in the
interpretation of PR 31f. Here see my essay, "Neville on the One and the Many," *Southern
Journal of Philosophy* 10/1 (Spring, 1972), 79-84.
[18] See Hartshorne's essay, "Whitehead's Novel Intuition," pp. 18-26 in *Alfred North
Whitehead: Essays on His Philosophy*, ed. George L. Kline (Englewood Cliffs: Prentice-Hall,
1963), reprinted in WP, chapter 11.

in terms of God's primordial decision (let alone the decisions of finite occasions) or in terms of analytic *a priori* principles. No reason can be given because, paradoxically, it is the reason why actual entities are the only reasons. Every reason, by the ontological principle, is rooted in some decision, either the decisions of other occasions for that particular occasion, or in that occasion's own decision (PR 36f, 68). A decision indicates why something is so and not otherwise. Creativity underlies both the making of such decisions and the necessary availability of other decisions for such self-decision. It is the ultimate explanation for the ontological principle, and as such is exempt from its requirement that it have a more specific reason why it is so and not otherwise.[19] Ultimately, "the sole appeal is to intuition" (PR 32), but such intuition may be appraised in terms of the success or failure of Whitehead's metaphysics as a whole.

In contrast to my sharp differentiation between our two thinkers with respect to the nature of metaphysical principles, William M. O'Meara's essay in this monograph sees Hartshorne's metaphysical method to be a natural extension of Whitehead's approach.

This very able defense turns on Hartshorne's conception of metaphysics as the study of nonrestrictive existential affirmations. A metaphysical principle must be consistent with the existence of any experience (hence nonrestrictive) and be exemplified in every possibility capable of actualization (thus existential, in contrast to logic and mathematics). Now there can be only one set of consistently conceivable principles which are both nonrestrictive and affirmatively existential. Hartshorne therefore argues that all other proposed metaphysical systems must be inconsistent. They claim to be existential, capable of actualization, and yet they are inconsistent with those metaphysical principles we independently hold to be true and hence applicable to whatever is capable of actualization. But a false metaphysical system might just be internally self-consistent even if inconsistent with these conditions for actualization.

Rather than holding alternative metaphysical systems to be false because inconsistent, as Hartshorne does, we may regard them to be false because lacking existential exemplification. This approach enables us to conceive of a variety of consistent metaphysical systems, though only one is actualizable. Whatever metaphysical principles there are, they must be exemplified in every single actuality and in every possibility capable of actualization, and hence forever exclude their rivals.

This approach maintains Hartshorne's conception of metaphysics as the study of nonrestrictive existential statements, but includes negations as well as affirmations. Other internally consistent systems are studied by logic and mathematics, which prescind from questions of existence, since it is a contingent matter whether such systems are in fact instantiated in existence. But just as it is characteristic of true metaphysical principles

---

[19] See William J. Garland, "The Ultimacy of Creativity," *Southern Journal of Philosophy* 7/4 (Winter, 1969-70), 361-76

that they must always be exemplified, it is characteristic of false metaphysical principles that they can never be exemplified. Metaphysics should embrace the necessarily nonexistent (though conceivable) as well as the necessarily existent. In that case there are genuine, consistent metaphysical alternatives, and we must look to God's primordial decision for the ultimate reason why one is chosen rather than another, and to experience to discover which one in fact is actually being exemplified.

5. *Prehensions of Contemporaries.* Now that Hartshorne has abandoned his former contention that contemporaries can prehend one another, there is no longer any major difference with Whitehead on this point. Yet it is interesting to note that much of the motivation for his earlier stand stems from his assumption that God experiences the world in terms of successive temporal unifications. If God does not prehend contemporaries, then it would seem that the immediately present multiplicity of actual occasions would lie outside of God's present unification of his experience, first being included in the next successive divine occasion.

Hartshorne agrees with Whitehead that only being can be prehended, and that an actual occasion first achieves determinate being in satisfaction. Simultaneously with that satisfaction, on Whitehead's theory, the occasion is incorporated into the nontemporal unity of divine experience. For Hartshorne, on his present view, this inclusion into divine experience can only first take place in the next divine occasion, even though that occasion may be immediately contiguous to the satisfied actual occasion. Whitehead does not need the prehension of contemporaries, which would be a help to Hartshorne were it possible, simply because God does not prehend any occasions from standpoints other than their own and needs no temporal standpoint of his own from which to unify his experience.

6. *Perishing and Objective Immortality.* Whitehead argues that the temporal unification of the actual world in present experience entails perspectival elimination (PR 517), but it is not clear whether this is simply an empirical fact or a metaphysical necessity. Hartshorne, championing divine temporal unification, urges the former. Further, in line with his axiom that "to be (or to be true or false) is to be capable of being known somehow,"[20] particularly by God, he insists that nothing of the immediacy of the occasion is lost in God's prehension of it. Differences on this latter point stem largely from differences in the interpretation of Whitehead, not in metaphysical differences deriving from Hartshorne's temporalistic restriction, though Griffin notes that his earlier doctrine of the prehension of contemporaries may have strongly influenced this interpretation.

The claim that finite entities retain their subjective immediacy in their objective immortality in God seems to have a different meaning to Hartshorne than to his critics. To me it means that each of my former selves is still experiencing whatever it experienced as caught up in the life of God. It

---

[20] Eugene H. Peters, *Hartshorne and Neoclassical Metaphysics*, p. 115.

means that one of the subjects in the life of George Washington is now still experiencing the crossing of the Delaware, that Julius Caesar is now still experiencing the crossing of the Rubicon, and Moses the crossing of the Sea of Reeds. But Hartshorne denies subjective immortality; is it *because* God now has these experiences that Washington, Caesar, and Moses do not? But insofar as occasions are in process of becoming, they necessarily enjoy subjectivity, and were it possible for such process of becoming to be included within the ongoing, everlasting experience of God, those occasions would continue to enjoy their subjectivity even as caught up in God.

Whitehead's argument is that the process of becoming, as that which is not determinate because it is a process of determination, is not prehendable. In prehending all the being experienced in the occasion's satisfaction, God "loses nothing that can be saved" (PR 525). What cannot be saved in divine consequent prehension is the occasion's subjectivity inherent in its process of becoming, for objective immortality cannot in itself confer subjective immortality. God prehends all occasions in their full immediacy of being, for there is no perishing of being in God insofar as this means "the fading of immediacy as events cease to be present events."[21] But there is the perishing of becoming, which cannot be prehended by God because it is not prehendable.

Basically, what I find missing in Hartshorne's account is just this contrast between being and becoming. His own contrast is somewhat different. Against the substance tradition which treats becoming as a deficient mode of being, Hartshorne insists that being is only an abstraction from becoming, which is reality itself. The dynamic, the mutable, includes the static, the immutable, as its abstract component. This argument is perfectly valid, to be sure, but only when applied to persistence through change. The being which persists unchanged through a series of changes is indeed abstract for both thinkers. We need only think of the defining characteristics of Whitehead's societies of occasions. But the being of a single individual occasion is fully concrete. Perhaps it is inappropriate to term such being static, since we normally reserve stasis to mean endurance or persistence over time (requiring a series of occasions, not just one), but we cannot conceive of the being of an individual occasion as dynamic either, for this would assign contradictory predicates to one and the same being, as G. H. von Wright has pointed out.[22] For all such dynamism requires that some property the being first had is now different. Hartshorne's becoming is the concreteness of successive occasions contrasted with elements of endurance, but this for Whitehead is change, not becoming. Becoming for Whitehead is neither concrete nor abstract (which are rather properties of being) but concrescence. To be sure, becoming includes being in the sense that each concrescing occasion prehends past being, but it is also true that such becoming is included in the being into which it concresces. Becoming is the process of determination which terminates in determinate being, which could not be what it is apart from such becoming.

This is the "principle of process" (PR 34f), but Hartshorne interprets it to mean that "the entity *is* its activity"[23] or that "process, as including its own past and abstract aspects, is the reality itself" (CSPM 109f). The activity, the happening, the occurring of an occasion is its being (since occasions, unlike houses, molecules, and rabbits, are not enduring entities), but such being is quite determinate and prehendable, unlike the process of becoming which constituted such reality. Subjectivity for Whitehead is wholly bound up in this becoming, a process which naturally terminates in the determinate being it is creating. "Completion is the perishing of [subjective] immediacy: 'It never really is'" (PR 130) and hence is never prehendable. Becoming "perishes" in being as determination terminates in determinateness, unification in unity.

Actual entities become and "perish, but do not change; they are what they are" (PR 52). Becoming, while it constitutes being, is not itself being, lacking both unity and determinateness. It prehends, but is not prehendable. Just because it is not being does not mean that it is nothing. Being contrasts with becoming as well as with nothing.

Unfortunately, Whitehead never made explicit the difference between the perishing of becoming and the perishing of being. The perishing of (subjective) becoming is natural and inevitable in the creation of (objective) being. Being, however, persists in being what it is except insofar as it is eliminated by means of negative prehensions. The physical unification of past being by temporal actual occasions requires negative prehension, both for spatiotemporal perspectival elimination and for the evasion of past evil (PR 517). But in God there is no loss or perishing of being since he positively prehends all that is prehendable. In this sense immediacy is retained, as Griffin points out, but not the original subjectivity of that immediacy.

7. *Genetic Succession: Real or Logical?* Hartshorne's denial of real genetic succession within concrescence is a strong contributory reason for his denial of any perishing of becoming (subjective immediacy) in God. Genetic succession is the way in which Whitehead explains becoming as a process of determination whereby incomplete phases of multiple feelings are successively reduced to the one, complete, determinate unity of feeling which is the satisfaction. At that juncture the indeterminacy of becoming gives way to the determinateness of being. If there is no such succession of indeterminate phases contrasting with the final determinate satisfaction, it is difficult to see how becoming can be understood as the creation of determinate being, or be that which must perish in order for being to be. In that case, Hartshorne's denial of any perishing in God would be fully justified. Hartshorne comments:

[23] "Whitehead's Novel Intuition," p. 22 (WP 165).

> When we are told that the indeterminacy of the actuality's self-creative process has "evaporated" with the achieving of a determinate satisfaction, this only means, I take it, that the particular resolution of the indeterminacy is henceforth definitive; i.e., the "decision" cannot be made over again or otherwise. But the process of deciding is not done away with, since it *is* the actual entity, and this, we are expressly told, can never change.[24]

But just what is this process of deciding on Hartshorne's view? Since he agrees with von Wright's argument that a being cannot have contradictory predicates, his process, to be both dynamic and prehendable, must refer to a succession of occasions: the same occasion cannot both be "undecided" and "decided." Yet in a Whiteheadian context the process of decision refers to the becoming or concrescence of a single occasion, in which what is undecided in earlier phases becomes decided in the later. Moreover, it is just such decision which is the core meaning of actuality (PR 68). Hartshorne is deprived this understanding of actuality since his decisions necessarily lack the unity of a single occasion.

The cogency of Whitehead's approach hinges on whether he can successfully reinterpret the conventional assumption that if A is earlier than B, then if B is present, A must lie in B's past, or if A is present, B must lie in A's future. Since each epochal occasion is temporally "thick," it may have successive layers of phases, each earlier or later than the others, but all compresent to one another as constitutive of the same moment.[25]

Hartshorne's rejection of this approach, it must be conceded, is independent of his temporalistic restriction denying the existence of any nontemporal actuality. But it is symptomatic of his resoluteness in insisting upon strict temporality in all instances, including those instances which Whitehead sought to understand in other ways, or which he was tempted to deny take place in physical time at all. Whitehead has a large arsenal of concepts in terms of which to come to grips with process, which Hartshorne tends to sweep aside in favor of a single, uniform temporal progression of unit-occasions.

III. ADDITIONAL DIFFERENCES

Let us consider four additional differences, apparently not explicitly noted by Hartshorne, which stem largely from the divergent views on possibility:

1. *The Laws of Nature.* In chapter 7 of *Adventures of Ideas*, Whitehead discusses four theories concerning the laws of nature without directly making a decision among them, though his own position is fairly easily ascertainable. The primary contrast concerns the first two theories, law as im-

---

[24] *Ibid.*, p. 22 (WP 166).

[25] This claim is argued further in my essays "On Genetic Successiveness: A Third Alternative," *Southern Journal of Philosophy* 7/4 (Winter, 1969-70), 421-25, and on "Genetic and Coordinate Division Correlated," *Process Studies* 1/3 (Fall, 1971), 199-209.

manent and law as imposed, and it is law as immanent which is compatible with his metaphysics. Immanent law means that "the order of nature expresses the characters of the real things which jointly compose the existences to be found in nature" (AI 142). Five consequences are mentioned: (1) scientists can seek for explanations and not merely for descriptions, (2) exact conformation of nature to any law is not to be expected, (3) since the laws depend on the characters of things, as they change, the laws will change, (4) immanence of law justifies a limited trust in induction, and (5) immanent law requires some doctrine of internal causal relatedness (AI 143f). The characters of things are causally inherited, and the laws of nature simply record the regularities of such inherited behavior, regularities not always fully obeyed and regularities open to evolutionary development. Imposed law, in contrast, involves a certain kind of Deism, for it needs "the correlative doctrine of a transcendent Deity," and is associated with external relations, independent substances, fixed and definite laws, and simple location (AI 144-46, 200f). Little of this, needless to say, squares with Whitehead's philosophy.

To be sure, Whitehead adds this comment:

Lastly apart from some notion of imposed law, the doctrine of immanence provides absolutely no reason why the universe should not be steadily relapsing into lawless chaos [in accordance with entropy, treating the world as a closed system, cut off from God]. In fact, the Universe, as understood in accordance with the doctrine of Immanence, should exhibit itself as including a stable actuality whose mutual implication with the remainder of things secures an inevitable trend towards order. The Platonic "persuasion" is required. (AI 146f)

The only "imposition" this entails is God's ordering of the possibilities each actuality confronts, to which it may or may not respond. Insofar as the creatures respond to such divine persuasion, there will be a gain in richness of order, but the laws of nature themselves are simply statistical generalizations of the actual regularity of behavior, itself only indirectly influenced by God.

In contrast, Hartshorne holds the laws of nature are divinely imposed. "The only 'acts of God' we can identify (in spite of the lawyers) are the laws of nature."[26] "One of the chief merits of a theistic philosophy," in his eyes, is "that it can explain the outlines of the world-order, the laws of nature, as divine decrees" (CSPM 125). "God's power to have any logically possible world" should be defined "not as his freedom to choose that world, but as his freedom to choose the basic laws of such a world and his capacity adequately to know and thus in the most absolute sense possess whatever world results from the laws plus the choices of the creatures so far as left open by the divine choice" (CSPM 137).[27]

In part this follows from Hartshorne's understanding of God as

---

[26] *A Natural Theology for Our Time*, p. 102; cf. p. 120.

[27] Hence Hartshorne sometimes speaks as if God determines precisely how much freedom we shall have: *The Logic of Perfection*, pp. 203f, 231 (hereafter, LP); *The Divine Relativity*, pp. 24, 35-37, 142 (hereafter, DR); CSPM 237.

the principle of limitation. Since for him metaphysical principles have no fully conceivable alternatives, the principle of limitation cannot apply to metaphysical principles, but must apply to principles of more restricted application, the laws of nature. These have conceivable alternatives, and are not necessarily everlastingly exemplified (CSPM 138, LP 96), but are chosen by God for differing cosmic epochs. More importantly, I think this position follows from a reflection on the ways in which a Hartshornian God could influence the world. A divine society of occasions, assimilated as far as possible to the theory of finite actual occasions, would presumably influence the world in exactly the same way as do actual occasions: by being past actualities a nascent occasion must take into account in achieving its own concrescence. Past occasions restrict the freedom of creaturely activity by imposing limits upon what it can become, for it can only become that which incorporates the past "given" to it within itself. The limitation God imposes, however, will not be as localized and fragmentary as that of a single past actual occasion, but pervasive and fundamental. God acts, not in terms of his unchanging primordial nature, which is merely his abstract invariant essence, but in terms of his successive consequent states which impose the laws of nature appropriate to that cosmic epoch. God's action thereby limits creaturely freedom, but he seeks to establish those laws which will permit a maximum of freedom consistent with the prevention of any degeneration into simple chaos.

2. *Divine persuasion.* Hartshorne explains such divine imposition in terms of persuasion:

> Process would come to an end if limits were not imposed upon the development of incompatible lines of process. The comprehensive order of the world is enjoyed, but not determined or created, by ordinary actual entities. Since the particular order is logically arbitrary, it must be either a blind fact wholly opaque to explanation or the result of a synthesis which deliberately selected it.... A divine prehension can use its freedom to create, and for a suitable period maintain, a particular world order. This selection then becomes a "lure," an irresistible datum, for all ordinary acts of synthesis.[28]

Or, again:

> The radical difference between God and us implies that our influence upon him is slight, while his influence upon us is predominant.... Hence God can set *narrow* limits to our freedom; for the more important the object to the subject, the more important is its effect upon the range of possible responses. Thus God can rule the world and order it, setting optimal limits for our free action, by presenting himself as essential object, so characterized as to weight the possibilities of response in the desired respect. (DR 141f)

Thus far, save perhaps for the final clause, Hartshorne has been describing his own doctrine of divinely imposed law, but he immediately identifies this with Whiteheadian divine persuasion, which we take to be a radically different theory:

---

[28]"Whitehead's Novel Intuition," p. 21 (WP 164); also WP 133. For a perceptive analysis of divine power, somewhat tangential to the question of imposition versus persuasion, see WP 99f.

This divine method of world control is called "persuasion" by Whitehead and is one of the greatest of all metaphysical discoveries, largely to be credited to White- head himself. He, perhaps first of all, came to the clear realization that it is by molding himself that God molds us, by presenting at each moment a partly new ideal or order of preference which our unself-conscious awareness takes as object, and thus renders influential upon our entire activity.... Only he who changes him- self can control the changes in us by inspiring us with novel ideals for novel occasions. We take our cues for this moment by seeing, that is, feeling, what God as of this moment desiderates. (DR 142)

Save perhaps for the mention of control, this is an accurate ac- count of Whitehead's doctrine. The past actual world each occasion confronts limits but does not determine its own outcome. Within these limits there is a range of possible alternative outcomes which God evaluates in terms of its potential contribution to the final beauty of the world. The occasion inherits this order of preference with the divine appetition towards the best outcome possible under the cir- cumstances dictated by the past, but the creature is free to respond as it will, for it can decide to actualize *any* of these possible alterna- tives, even that one least valued by God. But insofar as it responds favorably to the divine urging, the divine aim at increase in intensity of order has been achieved.

This differs from Hartshorne's theory of divine persuasion in at least three ways: (a) the laws of nature consequent upon such re- sponses are immanent, not imposed; (b) the divine lure is not "irresist- ible," for the creature is free to actualize that possibility most contrary to the one most valued by God; (c) God sets no limits upon our freedom; those limits are entirely set by the past actual world. God's is the still small voice which can be more easily evaded, if de- sired, than any of the demands past actuality place upon us. It is frequently ignored. But God is patient and wins out in the long run, since any creative advance is dependent upon obedience to that divine call.

Divine persuasion in Whitehead's sense is not really available to Hartshorne, since he rejects any need for the eternal objects. As long as possibility is simply the indeterminate potentiality of the past bear- ing on an indicated spatiotemporal region in the future, there can be no definite formal possibilities for God to evaluate. More importantly, God is not needed for the purpose of supplying the world with the for- mal possibilities which can order this indeterminate potentiality. But for Whitehead, God persuades the world to respond to his urg- ings in the way in which he supplies the world with its formal pos- sibilities, without which nothing could become actual. God and the world supply one another's needs. God is rich in possibility, but deficient in actuality, acquiring temporal actuality from the world, while the world is rich in actuality, but deficient in possibility, acquir- ing all its possibility from God. This contrast is lost in Hartshorne's system, as is the proper contrast between finitude and infinity. Hartshorne's God, defined basically in terms of his consequent states, is at all times finite, even though this finitude is ever-expanding and always includes all the actuality that is or ever was. Whitehead's God, defined basically in terms of his nontemporal actuality, is infinite. Spinoza was correct in arguing that an infinite God could only create an infinite world, but wrong in identifying this world with the world of actuality rather than with the world of possibility. For actuality is incurably finite. The world God creates in creating himself is the infinite domain of possibility. Thus God is essentially the infinite wealth of possibility, acquiring finitude from the world, while the world is fundamentally finite, acquiring a measure of infinity from God.

In the first section we criticized John Cobb's retention of the entire realm of eternal objects when interpreted as the permanent, enduring possession of an everlasting society of divine occasions, preferring Hartshorne's reduction of the primordial nature to the bare abstract divine essence as that which alone deserved exemplification within God at all times. But Cobb's instinct in preserving the eternal objects was sound, for it enables him to make sense of divine persuasion in ways not open to Hartshorne. In particular, it is difficult to understand the religious significance of divine action on Hartshorne's view. God inspires our activities primarily by being the cosmic, all-inclusive recipient of all our actions, preserving and enjoying them forevermore, thereby rescuing them from the transiency of the world and endowing them with ultimate significance. The imposition of the laws of nature, however, seems deficient in religious inspiration, even if it is God's primary mode of acting. While we may be comforted and reassured that God thereby protects us from chaos, this is primarily a matter for physics rather than for ethics and religion. Whitehead's God, in contrast, is supremely worthy of worship because he is the dynamic source of all values. God inspires us primarily by what he contributes to us in the form of values for us to actualize. Our contribution to him is derivative, for it is dependent upon how we respond to his contribution to us. But there is no way to respond to a law of nature, particularly if imposed by God; it must simply be obeyed, willy-nilly, for we have no choice in the matter.

3. *The Nature of Subjectivity.* Divine persuasion is effected by providing each occasion with its initial subjective aim. God's evaluation of the alternative possibilities confronting the occasion provides, in the highest possibility which is invested with the divine appetition, the subjective ideal for the occasion's aim, the initial impetus for its creative process of unification. Creativity by itself is merely the drive of the many toward unity, but this drive is blind and must be guided by the subjective aim. The subject of the occasion actualizes itself through the decisions it makes in unifying the past multiplicity it has inherited in accordance with the subjective aim and in modifying that aim in accordance with the past inherited. Without

the subjective aim, there can be no creative unification, no self-actualiza-tion, no emergence of subjectivity.

In many ways the subjective aim is *the* distinctive mark of White-head's metaphysics. It is the occasion for an original and novel argu-ment for the existence of God, for God is primarily and almost exclusively invoked in the first four parts of *Process and Reality* as the only entity capable of supplying the initial subjective aims. Only Whitehead seems to have taken the problem of the origin of subjectivity seriously (except per-haps Sartre), and to have seen the need for a divine source for the emerg-ence of subjectivity. Naturalistic Whiteheadians, such as Donald W. Sherburne, recognize the centrality of subjective aim even in their efforts to do away with the God whose chief metaphysical function is to provide such initial subjective aims.

Very little of this, however, is apparent in Hartshorne's philosophy. There can be no subjective aim as such in a Hartshornian occasion because it has no definite ideal possibility functioning as an ordering and unifying principle whereby the indeterminate, multiple potentiali-ties of the past can be reduced to unity. Presumably, it has no need for such a unifying principle, but this may be simply an argument from necessity, since there are no formal possibilities available to function in this role. Subjectivity seems to signify the self-creativeness of the occasion, the final determination it makes over and above the determinations of the causal past to render itself fully actual. If so, subjectivity is simply another name for the creativity instanced in that particular occasion.

These comments must remain somewhat conjectural, for Hart-shorne has written very little, to my knowledge, analyzing concres-cence. Without subjective aim or genetic succession, an analysis such as *Process and Reality*, part III, hardly seems likely. Hartshorne ap-pears to understand becoming on the metaphor of a continuous motion, somewhat like Bergson. The occasion is the smallest unit of such process, and the "completion of process" signifies that this move-ment has reached its terminus. The completion then is simply the final increment of the movement, which cannot affect or alter the movement up to that increment, as might be supposed to occur in the "perishing" of becoming. From Whitehead's perspective, such a "becoming" is simply the unfolding of a determinate process; what needs explaining is precisely how this process achieves its determinate character. Put another way: only that which is determinate can be persistent, can be the sort of thing capable of resisting "perishing," but determinate being, whether static or dynamic, requires explan-ation as to how it came into being. Whitehead set out to rescue Bergson's *durée* from the charge of anti-intellectualism (PR vii), and this he achieves in large part by offering as full a rational account as is possible of the process of creative emergence in the genetic analysis of concrescence.

Far from being "to some extent a genuinely eclectic affair, not wholly pertinent to the central insight,"[29] as Hartshorne argues, the theory of eternal objects is a necessary ingredient for the full elucidation of Whitehead's novel intuition of creativity.

4. *Panpsychism.* In some broad sense of the term, both men are clearly panpsychists. Within this broad agreement, however, there are some subtle yet important differences. For Whitehead we must carefully distinguish between subjectivity, mentality, and consciousness. There may well be degrees of varying intensity and frequency of consciousness in various organisms, but there is a threshold below which occasions have no consciousness whatsoever. Consciousness involves an effective contrast between what is and what might be, requiring the complex integration assigned to intellectual feelings, beyond the capacity of occasions of simpler experience. Subjectivity, on the other hand, simply denotes the present immediacy of becoming, in contrast to the past objectivity of being. It admits of no degree whatsoever, belonging equally to every actuality. Only mentality is a matter of degree for all actualities. Once distinguished from subjectivity and consciousness, mentality signifies the measure of novelty achieved by an occasion in contrast to its physical repetition of the past.

Hartshorne's defense of panpsychism does not trade so much on these distinctions, speaking rather of degrees of awareness, or sentience. They may not be too far apart on the matter of consciousness, for Hartshorne recognizes that "consciously detected data are a narrow sub-class of data, by any reasonable theory of experience" (CSPM 81), while for Whitehead consciousness may be conceived of as a special type of high-grade mental activity. But the identification of subjectivity with becoming, and the contrast between the mental and the physical are missing. "The absolute opposite of infinite awareness is simply complete unawareness. What light is cast upon the zero point of mentality by calling it matter?"[30] None, perhaps, if mentality is primarily awareness; considerable, if it is novelty in contrast to habitual repetition.

Arthur O. Lovejoy has observed:

> One of the principal motives . . . of panpsychism in the philosophy of our own time is the desire to avoid the discontinuity which is manifestly implied by the supposition that consciousness or sentiency is an "emergent" property or function, which abruptly supervenes at a certain level of the integration of matter, and at a certain stage in planetary evolution. Underlying all such reasoning is the assumption of the necessity of what may be called the "retrotensive method"—the rule that whatever is empirically found in or associated with the more complex and highly evolved natural entities must inferentially be read back into the simpler and earlier ones.[31]

This approach is most pronounced in the thinking of Teilhard de Char-

---

[29] *Ibid.*, p. 20 (WP 163).
[30] *Beyond Humanism*, p. 170. See also WP 118f.
[31] *The Great Chain of Being* (Cambridge: Harvard University Press, 1936), pp. 276f.

din, whose guiding principle seems to be: whatever is emergent in the course of evolution must have already been latent in that from which it emerged. The whole universe is likened to one vast Aristotelian substance, endowed with an inner entelechy culminating in the Omega point. Here the potentiality invested in matter is enormous. In contrast, the potentiality simple occasions possess on Whitehead's view is quite modest. An occasion need only be capable of (a) unifying and reproducing the past, and (b) responding, to some degree, to divine initiative. As the reservoir of all formal possibilities, God provides each creature with that measure of novelty which on other theories must be assigned to an "active potentiality" received from the past. Hartshorne's view is somewhere in between. Against Teilhard he stresses the radical openness of the future. The potentiality in things is not directed toward a specific goal, and the course of the evolutionary process depends more upon the creative decisions of individual actualities. Nonetheless the continuity of all beings, with their varying degrees of awareness, must be emphasized, because there can be no fresh input of potentiality or possibility into the world. The denial of formal possibilities or eternal objects precludes this.

In addition to these four differences, there is a difference between their characteristic approaches to the way in which we have philosophical knowledge of God. Hartshorne conceives of a single class of actualities, the actual occasions, understanding God as the everlasting, all-inclusive personal society of divine actual occasions. Here the logic of perfection is paramount: God is known by carefully conceiving the nature of actuality in its highest and best form. Moreover, since finite actualities differ from God only contingently, natural theology and metaphysics coincide. Hartshorne can therefore assert that "the idea of God, fully developed, is the entire content of non-empirical knowledge (including arithmetic and formal logic). Neither Peirce nor Whitehead say this with any explicitness; there is nothing in metaphysics (or *a priori* knowledge) not also in natural theology. They are essentially the same."[32] Whitehead agrees that God's primordial envisagement embraces the entire content of non-empirical knowledge, but the contents of his knowledge are not identical with the systematic principles he exemplifies. As an actual entity God exemplifies all the metaphysical principles, but there is also a subordinate systematic contrast between God, the one, unique actual entity originating from its mental pole, and the World, the totality of finite, physical actual occasions. Since this systematic contrast necessarily derives from the general metaphysical principles, metaphysics embraces two sub-disciplines, natural theology and cosmology, whose contents are necessarily distinct. Thus God is known in terms of categoreal exemplification understood by means of this systema-

---

[32] "The Development of My Philosophy," pp. 223f in *Contemporary American Philosophy: Second Series*, ed. John E. Smith (London: George Allen & Unwin, 1970).

tic contrast, not primarily in terms of the logic of perfection. We have commented sufficiently on this difference elsewhere.[33]

[33] "Process Philosophy and Our Knowledge of God," in *Traces of God in a Secular Culture,* ed. George F. McLean, O.M.I. (New York: Alba House, 1973). See also fn. 13.

CHAPTER V

HARTSHORNE'S INTERPRETATION OF WHITEHEAD'S METHODOLOGY

William M. O'Meara

Hartshorne identifies himself as an interpreter of Whitehead who has recognized a problem in Whitehead's claim that the philosopher can attain *necessary truths* by the method of *description of experience.*[1] In order to solve this problem of how metaphysical truths may be both experiental (i.e., *descriptive*) and *necessary*, Hartshorne proposes a notion of metaphysical truth based on logical consistency. "Metaphysical truths may be described as such that no experience can contradict them, but also such that any experience must illustrate them."[2] He defends logical consistency with every experience as the criterion of *a priori* metaphysical truth by distinguishing three kinds of statements: (1) those partially restrictive of existential possibilities; (2) those completely restrictive; and (3) those completely non-restrictive.

(1) Partially restrictive statements are illustrated by ordinary factual statements. If they are affirmative, they implicitly deny something, thereby restricting some existential possibility from being realized at the same time and place; and if they are negative, they implicitly affirm something. For example, to affirm that there are men in the room is to deny implicitly that the room is totally filled with air; and to deny that there are men in the room is to affirm implicitly that every part of the room contains something other than a man.[3]

(2) A completely restrictive statement is one such as "Nothing exists," which would exclude anything and everything from existing. This statement restricts any existential possibility from being realized. Consequently, such a statement is unverifiable, since the verifying statement itself would have to exist. Also, such a statement is falsifiable since the

---

[1] See "Whitehead and Contemporary Philosophy," p. 35, in *The Relevance of Whitehead,* edited by Ivor Leclerc (New York: Macmillan, 1961), reprinted in *Whitehead's Philosophy: Selected Essays, 1935-1970,* p. 153. For Whitehead's claim, see *Religion in the Making,* p. 88, and *Process and Reality,* pp. 3-6 (hereafter PR).

[2] "Some Empty Though Important Truths," *Review of Metaphysics* 8/4 (June, 1955), 553-68, quoting from p. 557. Reprinted in *The Logic of Perfection,* pp. 280-97, quoting from p. 285 (hereafter, LP).

[3] "Metaphysical Statements as Non-Restrictive and Existential," *Review of Metaphysics* 12/1 (September, 1958), 35-47, quoting from p. 35. Hereafter cited as "Metaphysical Statements."

existence of any experience at all falsifies the statement. Accordingly, a completely restrictive statement is impossible to verify and always falsifiable since it is not consistent with the existence of any experience. Hartshorne suggests that such completely restrictive statements should be viewed as expressing "impossibility" and not "a conceivable but unrealized fact."[4]

(3) A completely non-restrictive statement is one which is consistent with the existence of any experience. Such a statement would be, "Something exists." Since this is the contradictory of the completely restrictive statement, "Nothing exists," it should be necessarily true. For a completely restrictive statement is impossible, and the contradictory of an impossible statement is necessary. In contrast to the completely restrictive statement which was unverifiable and always falsifiable, the completely non-restrictive statement is always verifiable and unfalsifiable. The statement, "Something exists," is unfalsifiable and always verifiable since the supposed falsifying experience would itself have to exist and would thereby verify it rather than falsify it. Consequently, a metaphysical truth as a completely non-restrictive statement is to be discerned through its properties of being unfalsifiable and always verifiable by any experience.[5]

Hartshorne views metaphysics as studying non-restrictive, existential affirmations in contrast to mathematics which studies non-restrictive, non-existential affirmations. Mathematical statements as usually interpreted affirm, not that something with a certain character exists, but that if it did, such and such would also be the case. Mathematics only explores relations between possibilities without affirming that any particular possibility exists. In contrast, metaphysics tries to identify those possibilities which cannot be unexemplified. Metaphysics explores being *qua* being, namely, the strictly universal features of the ultimate realities, those features which must be exemplified, such as the statement, "Something exists."[6]

Since the proposition "Something exists," is necessary, Hartshorne argues that the contemporary dogma is wrong which asserts that a statement is rendered contingent by the mere fact that it asserts existence. For the false dogma, "all existential statements are contingent," the following true principle should be substituted, "all partially restrictive statements are contingent and all completely non-restrictive statements are necessary."[7] The criterion for a metaphysical truth is whether or not positive illustration of the proposition is inconsistent with, that is, would exclude, anything positive. This criterion of *a priori* metaphysical truth may be incapable of clear and certain application by man's cognitive powers. But such a difficulty would not make metaphysical truth un-

[4] *Ibid.*
[5] *Ibid.*, pp. 35f.
[6] *Ibid.*, pp. 35-37.
[7] *Ibid.*

knowable in itself. For what is common to all possible worlds is certainly
included in the present actual world; it is only a matter of trying to identify
the metaphysical elements, which again may be quite difficult.[8]

Hartshorne's proposal for determining metaphysical truth in an *a
priori* way through consistency with every possible experience is in fundamental agreement with Whitehead's comments on metaphysics and
consistency. For Whitehead does hold that metaphysical truths are necessary truths which apply to every possible and actual experience (PR 5f).
Further, Whitehead agrees with basing logic upon the concept of consis-
tency/inconsistency. Inconsistency introduces Spinoza's concept of finitude. The finite reality is necessarily inconsistent with some other state
of affairs, since the finite reality of the square, for example, cannot be at
the same time a circle. Inconsistency as the basis for logic is a fundamental principle of Whitehead's metaphysical understanding of reality
in process. By means of process, the universe can escape from the exclu-
sions of finite inconsistency.[9]

In summary, a metaphysical proposition for Whitehead is necessarily
true, describing every possible and actual experience; but the non-metaphysical proposition is contingently true, not applicable to all experiences.
For example, the two non-metaphysical propositions, one describing the
shape of a circle and the other the shape of a square, cannot both be applicable to the same experience. The non-metaphysical proposition excludes
the simultaneous realization of some other meaningful proposition, whereas the metaphysical proposition does not exclude such realization. Accordingly, Hartshorne agrees with Whitehead in proposing that partially
restrictive propositions, that is, ordinary factual statements, are contingently true, whereas completely non-restrictive propositions, that is, metaphysical statements exemplifiable by any possible experience, are necessarily true.

However, Hartshorne's *a priori* method for discovering metaphysical
truths might appear to violate Whitehead's use of the method of the working hypothesis. For Whitehead, metaphysics should avoid the dogmatic
fallacy, the belief that the beginning points of reflection are clear, obvious,
and irreformable.[10] But Hartshorne argues that all metaphysical truths are
implied by the fundamental, metaphysical truth, "Something exists." He
seems to be saying that a simple analysis of that proposition will disclose
within itself all other metaphysical truths.[11] However, that procedure is not
what Hartshorne is proposing, but rather experimentation with meanings
of propositions to discover those propositions which are completely non-
restrictive. He explicitly rejects the fallacious notion that insights into the
absolute must be absolute insights, that is, that insights into metaphysical

[8] "Some Empty Though Important Truths," pp. 557f (LP 285).
[9] Whitehead, *Modes of Thought*, pp. 72f.
[10] *Adventures of Ideas*, p. 287.
[11] "Metaphysical Statements," p. 37.

truths must be unqualified insights. Any insight into a metaphysical truth should be accepted not as an absolute, never to be reconsidered, but rather as an hypothesis to be considered in the light of its deductive implications and of how well it fits into all human experience. Accepted as hypotheses, such insights should be defended against a vigorous devil's advocate. Such insights should be expanded by deduction as a way of testing the insights by examining the self-evidence and testability of their consequences. Hartshorne's procedure is to experiment with such insights by trying to find those which are *a priori* consistent in mutually implying each other and in being completely non-restrictive and which are exemplified *a posteriori* in all experiences.[12] Therefore, Hartshorne's procedure does embody the Whiteheadian method of the working hypothesis.

Hartshorne's exemplification of his method should help to clarify his procedure. For example, he proposes that the following two propositions are completely non-restrictive, i.e., metaphysically true, and mutually imply each other, "Something exists," and "Experience occurs." The first statement has already been elucidated. The second statement, "Experience occurs," is in principle unfalsifiable and always verifiable by any existent experience since the experience itself exists. The statement does not appear to exclude any existential possibility. For "experience" is not to be taken in the sense of human or animal experience but in the metaphysical sense which Hartshorne and Whitehead propose. The existence of human experience would exclude during that time the existential realization of a world without human experience, but the existence of experience itself does not exclude any possible state of affairs from occurring. For in the Whiteheadian view, an act of experience is an appropriate way of conceptualizing actual entities, the ultimately real things which constitute the world (PR 28). Accordingly, Hartshorne concludes that this line of thought "strongly suggests, and I think proves that it [the statement "Experience occurs"] is necessarily true, or an *a priori* valid statement. . . . I conclude, that if the statement . . . is restrictive, there is no way to ascertain this. I think it is non-restrictive, and so necessary."[13]

Hartshorne's tentative conclusion about the statement is appropriate since the statement presupposes that the concept of experience can be generalized from human and animal experience to an analogous concept, a metaphysical factor, consistent with every possible state of affairs. The devil's advocate in the court of metaphysical inquiry should attack such a presupposition, and Hartshorne would be required to defend it at some length. A convincing defense, for example, would have to show how such a generalization would help make emergent evolution intelligible, as Whitehead attempts in *The Function of Reason*. Without such a defense, the Whiteheadian metaphysician cannot be sure that the generalization is

[12] *Man's Vision of God*, p. 68f (hereafter MVG); *A Natural Theology for Our Time* pp. 29f (hereafter, NTT).

[13] "Metaphysical Statements," pp. 38f.

adequate for the interpretation of any possible state of affairs (PR 4). Unless Hartshorne tests the application of the generalization to a state of affairs in which human and animal experience would not occur, he must face the difficulty that his criterion of *a priori* metaphysical truth may be incapable of clear and certain application to the statement "Experience occurs." The criterion of *a priori* metaphysical truth, defended by Hartshorne, is that a proposition is metaphysical if it describes a non-self-contradictory concept which is completely non-restrictive of any possible state of affairs. The abstract application of this criterion to the concept "Experience occurs," is not sufficient for judging it to be metaphysically true.[14] For the mind is left with the desire that verification be had in which the concept is actually seen to be applied meaningfully to various different states of affairs.

In the light of these reflections, Hartshorne's procedure for determining metaphysical truth by an *a priori* criterion is a valid Whiteheadian development of the method of the working hypothesis; but Hartshorne's procedure needs to be supplemented by the inductive method Whitehead himself used. It is in this light that Hartshorne's methodological commitment to the redoing of Anselm's ontological argument must be judged.[15] Hartshorne's redoing of the argument is valid according to his Whiteheadian criterion of metaphysical truth as completely non-restrictive. In fact, it would be a disconfirmation of Whitehead's theism if it were impossible *a priori* to form a concept of Whitehead's God as a noncontradictory possibility which was completely non-restrictive (NTT 33f). However, as Hartshorne himself points out, the whole burden of asserting the existence of God as a metaphysical truth should not be placed on the ontological argument, since other approaches are available in Whiteheadian metaphysics. All such approaches, including the ontological argument, should be used as mutually confirming each other (MVG 339f).

---

[14] *Ibid.*, p. 12.
[15] *Ibid.*, p. 47.

CHAPTER VI

Relativity Theory and Hartshorne's Dipolar Theism

FREDERIC F. FOST

From the earliest period of his writing, Charles Hartshorne has been continually perplexed by the difficulty of reconciling his doctrine of God with the fundamental tenets of relativity physics.[1] The problem has been a particularly acute one for Hartshorne because for a number of years he developed his neoclassical theism in a manner that involved two correlative notions reminiscent of Newtonian physics: the mutual immanence of contemporary events and an absolute cosmic simultaneity.[2] Both of these controversial points were maintained in sharp contrast to the consensus in present-day physics that (1) there is no causal relatedness between contemporary events, and (2) the idea of a simultaneous cross section of the universe has no clear meaning at all.[3]

Hartshorne was of course not unaware of the tremendous difficulty of reconciling the creative advance of the world with the denial by relativity

[1] "Whitehead's Idea of God," in *The Philosophy of Alfred North Whitehead*: The Library of Living Philosophers, ed. Paul A. Schilpp (Evanston and Chicago: Northwestern University, 1942), pp. 545f, reprinted in *Whitehead's Philosophy: Selected Essays, 1935-1970* (hereafter, WP), pp. 86f. Review of *Whitehead's Theory of Knowledge* by John Blyth in *Philosophy and Phenomenological Research* 3/3 (March, 1943), 375. In "The Divine Relativity and Absoluteness: A Reply," *The Review of Metaphysics* 4/1 (September, 1950), 60, Hartshorne wrote: "I am greatly troubled by the problem of contemporaries which leads straight into questions about 'physical' relativity where I always seem to become confused." See also *A Natural Theology for Our Time* (hereafter, NTT), p. 93.

[2] "On Some Criticisms of Whitehead's Philosophy," *The Philosophical Review* 44/4 (July, 1935), 334 (WP 31); "The Compound Individual," in *Philosophical Essays for Alfred North Whitehead* (New York: Longmans, Green and Co., 1936), p. 209 (WP 53); "The Interpretation of Whitehead (Reply to John W. Blyth)," *The Philosophical Review* 48/4 (July, 1939), 422f; Review of *Whitehead's Theory of Knowledge*, p. 375; "Is Whitehead's God the God of Religion?" *Ethics* 53/3 (April, 1943), 222 (WP 103); "The Divine Relativity and Absoluteness: A Reply," p. 59; "Absolute Objects and Relative Subjects: A Reply," *The Review of Metaphysics* 50/1 (September, 1961), 182f; *Man's Vision of God and the Logic of Theism* (hereafter, MVG), p. 287f.

[3] For an excellent comparative analysis of the differences between Newtonian and Einsteinian physics, see Milič Čapek, *The Philosophical Impact of Contemporary Physics* (Princeton: Van Nostrand Co., Inc., 1961). Both John Wilcox ("A Question from Physics for Certain Theists," *Journal of Religion* 40/4 [October, 1961], 293-300), and Lewis S. Ford ("Is Process Theism Compatible with Relativity Theory?" *Journal of Religion* 48/2 [April, 1968], 124-35) have explored the difficulties of reconciling Hartshorne's theism with relativity physics.

physics of an absolute simultaneity.[4] He admitted that relativity theory does not allow for instantaneous activity on a pervasive cosmic scale, and he acknowledged this to be "a serious complication" though not "an insuperable difficulty" for his position (LP 205 n6). He conceded that the problem of correlating the divine time of cosmic becoming with worldly time as understood by contemporary physical theory is "a neglected and apparently extremely formidable task."[5]

Relativity considerations aside, however, Hartshorne's panentheistic conception of God as all-inclusive of the world seemed to require both of these notions as corollaries of the divine omniscience. Hence, in spite of the difficulties involved, Hartshorne maintained that the conflict between his dipolar theism and relativity physics is only an "apparent" one. "Somehow relativity as an observational truth must be compatible with divine unsurpassibility."[6]

Sometime during the decade of the fifties a very interesting shift took place in Hartshorne's thought: he completely reversed his position on contemporary relations. While in 1950 he could still admit (though with some misgivings) that there must be real relations between contemporary happenings,[7] by 1964 his new position was clear. "Since an event can, on my view, be intrinsically related to another only by having it as datum, and it scarcely seems that two events can each be datum for the other, it appears that contemporaries . . . cannot have intrinsic relatedness."[8]

Nevertheless, even after he had given up his earlier doctrine of contemporary relations, he still continued to defend the notion of a cosmic simultaneity as an apparently indispensable aspect of his doctrine of God. The creative advance of the cosmos, he argued, implies a cosmic "front" of simultaneity. "I suppose God to have this cosmic now as his psychological simultaneity."[9]

As recently as 1970, however, Hartshorne appears to have made a second concession to relativity physics by hinting that the idea of God's

[4] *The Logic of Perfection and Other Essays in Neoclassical Metaphysics* (hereafter, LP), pp. xi, 204.

[5] "Present Prospects for Metaphysics," *The Monist* 47/2 (Winter, 1963), 205. In another place Hartshorne offers the "possibly wild suggestion" that the "big bang" theory of cosmic development may offer a solution to the problems raised by the spatial expanse of the universe: "the laws of nature may have been decided at a moment in the cosmic process when there was no such expanse." (*Creative Synthesis and Philosophical Method* [hereafter, CSPM], p. 125.)

[6] NTT 93. This comment exhibits the basic rationalism of Hartshorne's methodology, particularly his understanding of the questions regarding God's existence as fundamentally a matter of metaphysical necessity and not empirical fact. See "The Rationalistic Criterion in Metaphysics," *Philosophy and Phenomenological Research* 8/3 (March, 1948), 436-47, and "Metaphysics for Positivists," *Philosophy of Science* 2/3 (July, 1935), 287-303.

[7] "The Divine Relativity and Absoluteness: A Reply," p. 59.

[8] "Interrogations of Charles Hartshorne," in Sydney and Beatrice Rome, eds., *Philosophical Interrogations* (New York: Holt, Rinehart and Winston, 1964), p. 324.

[9] *Ibid.*, p. 324f.

unitary intuition of a cosmic simultaneity may have to be abandoned as well. Instead of speaking of "God now," as he had so frequently done in the past, he now proposes the language of "God here-now."

> . . . God as perceiving us now is a divine state or event; God as perceiving a state of some inhabitant of another planet is another divine event. The two events will be embraced in later divine events in which God perceives remote descendants both of us and of our far-off contemporaries. (CSPM 123f)

Hartshorne realizes that if "God here-now" is not the same concrete reality as "God somewhere else now," then the analogy between the linear succession of states in the cosmic individual and those of localized individuals is severely compromised (CSPM 124). This is no small admission on Hartshorne's part, since he had earlier insisted that "the unity of our experience is the unity in which everything is initially found, and only by abstraction from or analogy with this unity can we understand *any* concrete unity."[10]

Even though Hartshorne is obviously troubled by the implications which relativity considerations introduce into the idea of the divine individuality ("It is a little like the mysteries of the trinity, only incomparably more complex") (CSPM 124), he still holds his ground with the assertion that the difficulties are really to be expected when an analogy is extended to include deity. "Maybe it is not divine individuality that is threatened, but only the assumption that this individuality should be simple and easy for us to grasp" (CSPM 124). The haunting question still remains: "Can physics, judging reality from the standpoint of localized observers, give us the deep truth about time as it would appear to a non-localized observer?" (CSPM 124f).

On the basis of the scanty evidence presently available, it is difficult to know whether Hartshorne has really given up his position on cosmic simultaneity. It does seem clear, however, that rejection of cosmic simultaneity would consistently follow from his denial of contemporary relatedness. To put it somewhat differently, one of the basic reasons why he was so reluctant to jettison the doctrine of contemporary relations was that even if he conceded that contemporaries are externally related to one another, they nevertheless seem to have the relation of coexistence or co-occurrence. Such a relation, if not real in terms of the events in question, must be real in the mind of God which considers them. Hence with reservation Hartshorne had to admit real relations between contemporary happenings.[11]

Since Hartshorne's dipolar theism was systematically developed within a framework which affirmed both contemporary relations and absolute simultaneity, it is hardly surprising that his subsequent denial of the former

---

[10] "Whitehead's Philosophy of Reality as Socially-Structured Process," *Chicago Review* 8/2 (Spring-Summer, 1954), 68; italics his (WP 117).

[11] "The Divine Relativity and Absoluteness: A Reply," p. 59.

and his apparent reconsideration of the latter should introduce incoherence into his system. In what follows we shall specifically focus attention on Hartshorne's reasons for earlier advocating a doctrine of contemporary relations and the implications which his subsequent shift of position have for his doctrine of God.

I

Present-day physics admits only two fundamental relations in the universe, causal succession and contemporary independence.[12] Contemporaneity is thus the absence of causal influence or relation. Two events are contemporary if neither is internal to the other. Internality is therefore an affair of the past. Contemporaries are externally related and hence mutually independent.[13]

Against this position and in spite of the difficulties involved, Hartshorne for a number of years affirmed an "unqualified inclusiveness of prehension."[14] At least two lines of reasoning can be found in support of this position. First, to say that contemporary events are external to one another seemed to violate Whitehead's "ontological principle," according to which everything, in order to be at all, must be in some actual unit of experience. If the relations between contemporaries were external to *all* actual entities, then such relations would seem to be nowhere at all and hence would lack the ontological requisite for being factors within experience.[15]

In the second place, such externality or absence of relation between contemporaries would lead, Hartshorne felt, to a form of vicious regress emphasized by Bradley against which there is no defense.

> For if entities are mutually external and are both concrete, then their relations can belong to neither of them nor to anything more concrete which embraces them; and we can only say that the terms have to the relations the relation of being actually related by them, and this obviously involves an endless regress of the kind which is vicious because it must end if the terms are to be related. (MVG 287f)

Hartshorne postulated a way in which such regress could be avoided. One might assert that if there is no real relation between contemporaries as such, they are nevertheless together and hence related in the divine actuality. This would seem to cancel out the asserted externality, for the consequent nature of God prehends the contemporaries, which in turn prehend the contents of the consequent nature. Therefore, each prehends the other without any lapse of time.[16] In short, if all occasions are im-

---

[12] Čapek, *The Philosophical Impact of Contemporary Physics*, pp. 214-22.

[13] Cf. Whitehead, *Adventures of Ideas*, p. 251 and *Process and Reality*, p. 345.

[14] "On Some Criticisms of Whitehead's Philosophy," p. 334 (WP 31).

[15] "Whitehead's Theory of Knowledge," p. 375.

[16] "Whitehead's Theory of Knowledge," p. 375. Cf. "Is Whitehead's God the God of Religion?" p. 222 (WP 103).

manent in God, and he in turn is immanent in them, are they not, then, immanent in each other?[17] "For, since God is not spatially separated from things, it seems no definite lapse of time can occur either between his prehension of them or theirs of him."[18]

In *The Divine Relativity* Hartshorne continued to defend the need for a mutual immanence among contemporary events, although one is now more cognizant of the growing difficulty he had of reconciling contemporary relations with his virtually axiomatic insistence that time has an asymmetrical structure.

> The particular, succeeding subject prehends the more general, preceding object; and this relation relativizes the particular prehender to the prehended, the successor to the predecessor, the particular to the general, but *not* conversely.[19]

Nevertheless, Hartshorne cleverly proposed as an alternative to the above principle the notion that contemporary events may be mutually *interdependent*. If there is no *inter*action between present events and those of the past or future, then it seems that contemporaries must either have no action upon one another, or there must be *action both ways* (DR 99). Hartshorne was able to make this proposal from the standpoint of his pansubjective ontology. Suppose a subject S knows a contemporary C. According to Hartshorne's realistic epistemology, it is the subject that is relative to the object, the knower to the known, thus preserving the independence of the object. Hence this would not mean, of itself, any relativity of C to S. But Hartshorne suggests the possibility of a reverse relation of C to S other than the "non-genuine one" of C's merely being known by S. If C is another knowing subject, S[1], then there may be a mutual awareness between S and S[1].

> Each would enter into the other, not merely as knower but as known-knower. Everything known, even a knower of oneself as known, is constitutive of the knower by which it is known.[20]

As plausible as this alternative may have been, given the acceptability of panpsychism, Hartshorne evidently was not fully satisfied with the proposal. For immediately after the last sentence quoted he writes:

> The topic of contemporary relations bristles with difficulties, and I shall only say that *if* I could find a consistent analysis of it, I should be able to die content, so far as philosophical achievements are concerned. At present

[17] "Whitehead's Idea of God," p. 545 (WP 87).

[18] *Ibid.* This position, however, seemed to involve embarrassing consequences for Hartshorne in another vein. If God is contemporaneously related to events in their very act of becoming, then it would seem that his knowledge of a given event, which by definition is omniscient to the minutest detail, would preclude any internal freedom on the part of the event. As we shall see below, Hartshorne attempted to circumvent this difficulty by holding that two contemporary events may be *mutually determining* and hence each may be partly free in relation to the other.

[19] *The Divine Relativity* (hereafter, DR), p. 98; italics his.

[20] DR 99. See also *Reality as Social Process*, p. 76f.

the topic seems the most vulnerable point in the surrelativist doctrine. (DR 99)

The shift in Hartshorne's views on contemporary relations seems to have grown out of reflection on the logical structure of experience. Experience, Hartshorne holds, is always *of* something, the objective givenness of which is distinguishable from the experience in which it is given.[21] Moreover, there is no present self-contained event which is given as such, for "givenness is a causal and temporal arrow pointing backwards and outwards in space-time, and indeed it is an actual grasp of events whose beginning was independent of the present event."[22] In short, the subject-object structure is fundamentally the present-past structure. All direct awareness is memory of the past.[23] Only past events, which are fully determined, are ready to be experienced.[24]

II

We turn now to a discussion of the implications which are entailed by Hartshorne's shift of position regarding contemporary relations. Our argument may be formulated in the following thesis statements: (1) By relinquishing his earlier position concerning the mutual immanence of contemporary occasions and adopting the view that contemporaries are causally unrelated to one another, Hartshorne has undermined the fundamental idealistic axiom upon which his philosophical theology is built: namely, the assumption that to be is to be known by God, and that God's knowledge is not only the measure of reality but that it literally includes all reality. (2) When this basic idealistic assumption is called in question by a view of relations that allows for a contemporary world that is cognitively independent of the divine actuality, then several aspects of Hartshorne's doctrine of God (which were originally formulated so as to require for their intelligibility a cosmic contemporaneity) no longer appear to be defensible: (A) The description of the divine essence as the all-pervasive factor of reality becomes inconsistent with the affirmation of a contemporary world vis-à-vis the divine actuality. (B) Insofar as Hartshorne's formulation of the ontological argument is dependent upon the acceptance of the divine essence as co-extensive with all reality, it too becomes forfeit to an unacceptable inconsistency (on grounds quite distinct, it should be noted, from usual criticisms of his reformulation of the argument). (C) To the extent that the panentheistic principle of the inclusiveness of the divine actuality rests

---

[21] "The Logical Structure of Givenness," *The Philosophical Quarterly* 8 (October, 1958), 308.

[22] "The Structure of Givenness," *The Philosophical Forum* 18 (1960-1961), 37f.

[23] *Ibid.*, p. 37.

[24] "Hume's Metaphysics and Its Present-Day Influence," *The New Scholasticism* 35/2 (April, 1961), 162.

on Hartshorne's view of the omniscience of God, this must be amended to allow for a more clear-cut distinction between God and the world.

We turn now to a detailed examination of the first thesis statement above, after which we shall show the implications of denying that omniscience is the measure of reality for those aspects of Hartshorne's doctrine of God that are enumerated in statement two above.

Hartshorne's affinities with the idealistic epistemology of Berkeley and Royce have been clearly set forth in a number of his writings.[25] His position may be summarized in the following propositions: (1) Reality is to be defined in terms of experience or knowledge; (2) Because of the uncertainty, doubt, and inconsistency that render all human knowing imperfect, there is a non-coincidence of things as they are known by us and things as they are in themselves; (3) Human knowledge, therefore, cannot be regarded as an adequate measure of reality; (4) This awareness of the distinction between what we know and reality leads us to surmise the possibility of knowledge more perfect than ours; (5) Since our human knowing only partially fulfills such internal characteristics of knowledge as consistency, clarity and certainty, we are led to posit an ideal form of knowledge that entirely meets these criteria; (6) Reality must therefore be what the internally perfect knowledge has as its presented content; (7) If the real consists in its relation to the adequate knower, then to be is to be known by God.

My concern at this point is not to criticize the above propositions by offering an alternative set of assumptions, but rather to point out the internal incompatibility of the cumulative argument with the shift in Hartshorne's thought regarding contemporary relations. This may be done by analyzing several of Hartshorne's basic assumptions and then showing the inconsistency that obtains between them.

(1) Knowledge is a relation between the knower and the known, such that (A) the object term is externally related to the knower (that is, could have been what it is apart from that particular relation), while (B) the knower or subject term is genuinely (rather than nominally) related to the object term (that is, is constituted or made what it presently is by having relation to the object term).[26]

(2) Reality or the real is to be defined in terms of its relation to the fully adequate knower.

(3) Since the causal independence of contemporary events implies the *absence of relation* between them, God does not prehend the presently becoming world which is contemporary with him.

Now it follows that if the real is what is related to God [by assumptions

---

[25] "Royce's Mistake—and Achievement," *Journal of Philosophy* 53/3 (February 2, 1956), 123-30. "Ideal Knowledge Defines Reality: What Was True in Idealism," *Journal of Philosophy* 43/21 (October 10, 1946), 573-82.

[26] For an extended discussion of Hartshorne's doctrine of internal and external relations see the Appendix to Chapter II, "Relativity and Logical Entailment," in DR 95-115.

(1) and (2)], then *either* (A) there can be no contemporary, i.e., causally unrelated, world vis-à-vis the divine actuality [contrary to assumption (3)]; *or* (B) it is not the case that to be is to be known by God [contrary to (2)]. In short, we are left with two alternative disjunctions, one of which (A) is incompatible with Hartshorne's present views on contemporaneity, the other (B) with the essential idealistic foundation of his theism. Since Hartshorne's endorsement of contemporary independence is a needed concession to present-day physics, we maintain that consistency cannot be achieved at the expense of affirming the first disjunct. Hence we conclude that the second alternative is Hartshorne's only viable option, namely, that part of the real world, that which is in unison of becoming with God, is not known by God and consequently that omniscience cannot, without qualification, be said to be the measure of reality.

Now if the above line of reasoning can be sustained, then our conclusion has some significant implications for particular aspects of Hartshorne's doctrine of God. The dipolar theory of deity makes the distinction between the absolute and strictly necessary essence of God and his surrelative, contingent actuality. On the premise that the strictly necessary is necessitated by anything and everything,[27] Hartshorne holds that the divine essence is "the absolutely pervasive factor of reality."[28] God qua absolute is abstract constituent of all things, the universal common denominator of process as such.[29] In any possible state of affairs God will be included. He is thus the universally immanent ground of all things (MVG 53n5). "The sense in which God is part of each thing," Hartshorne writes,

> is that generalized sense better expressed as "factor of," meaning something in abstraction from which the thing would be less than it is. Now in abstraction from God, were such abstraction possible, we would be nothing, and that is certainly less than we are. So in that sense, God is a factor of everything, and he is precisely that one factor which alone sums up all that each thing is, and infinitely more besides. (MVG 285)

Another way in which Hartshorne describes the immanence of the divine essence is in terms of its unique status of being universal object-for-all-subjects (DR 70). To be known by all subjects is just as distinctive as knowing all objects. "Only God can be so universally important that no subject can ever wholly fail or ever have failed to be aware of him (in however dim or unreflective a fashion)" (DR 93, 98). In short, God as absolute, God in his essence, is being itself (DR 87f).

Now it is our contention that this view of the divine essence as immanently pervasive of the given actual world can be sustained only on the

---

[27] Hartshorne here follows Lewis' logic of strict implication, i.e., a necessary proposition is implied by any and every contingent proposition. See LP 56.

[28] "The Philosophy of Creative Synthesis," *Journal of Philosophy* 55/22 (October 23, 1958), 952f, italics his. See also LP 38, 43f, 65, 80f, 85, 98, 99f, where the same idea is developed under the notion of "universal existential tolerance."

[29] DR 70. Cf. "Absolute Objects and Relative Subjects: A Reply," p. 178 and "Whitehead's Philosophy of Reality as Socially-Structured Process," p. 65.

basis of the rejected assumption that omniscience is the measure of reality. That is to say, to affirm, as Hartshorne does, that the divine essence is the universally immanent and abstract constituent of all things is rendered intelligible only on the epistemological analogy of an infallible knower who prehends the presently becoming world which is contemporaneous with Him.

However, if the denial of contemporary relations entails a fundamental distinction between God and the world, such that God and the presently becoming world are mutually independent of one another, then Hartshorne's doctrine of the divine essence collapses along with the Berkeleyan foundation which was its *raison d'être*.

This may be illustrated by the following difficulty which arises, given Hartshorne's original view. If the divine essence is held to be coextensive with the world, then, on the assumption that contemporary events are causally unrelated, Hartshorne would in effect be making the embarrassing assertion that that which is contemporaneously independent of the divine actuality is nevertheless qualified by what is supposedly the defining characteristic of God's actuality—the divine essence itself! The only way in which Hartshorne can retain the view that the divine essence is coextensive with the actual world seems to be at the expense of once again affirming his rejected position regarding contemporary relations. In short, only two alternatives would appear to be open to Hartshorne if his doctrine of God is to remain internally coherent. Either (1) he must deny that God's essence is the absolutely pervasive factor of reality, or (2) he must surrender the notion of contemporary independence which makes it possible for there to be a world which is distinct from the divine actuality. Since the second alternative would undermine significant gains resulting from his shift in position, his only option seems to be a rejection of the view that God's essence is coextensive with the presently becoming universe.

Furthermore, since Hartshorne's doctrine of the divine essence is the distinctive element in the neoclassical reformulation of the ontological argument (LP 63f), it now becomes possible to take issue with the argument on an entirely different basis than the one used by most of Hartshorne's critics.

Only a dipolar theism such as Hartshorne's is able to overcome the logical type difficulty (the Findlay paradox) which turns the traditional Anselmian form of the ontological argument into a disproof.[30] By making a distinction between the contingent actuality and the necessary essence of deity, Hartshorne is able to counter the objection that from an abstract

[30] LP 24, 104; "Further Fascination on the Ontological Argument: Replies to Richardson," *Union Seminary Quarterly Review* 18/3, Part I (March, 1963), 245. This important discovery was made by J. N. Findlay, who, along with Sartre, is probably the only philosopher ever to have devised an *a priori* proof for the nonexistence of God. See "Can God's Existence Be Disproved?" *Mind* 57 (1948), 176; reprinted in Anthony Flew and A. MacIntyre, eds., *New Essays in Philosophical Theology* (London: SCM Press, 1955), pp. 47-56.

definition of God His concrete existence is illegitimately inferred. Since on Hartshorne's view the divine existence does not refer to God's concrete particularity but only to his abstract essence, it follows that the kind of "existence" which his form of the argument seeks to demonstrate has no reference to the concrete actuality of the divine individuality but only to the a priori necessity that the divine essence always be given some particular embodiment or other.[31] Hence it can now be seen that the defensibility of the argument ultimately rests upon Hartshorne's doctrine of the divine essence.

Now if the argument is concerned with the existential status of the divine essence rather than the divine actuality, it is obvious that such status must be unqualifiedly necessary, for the point of the argument is to demonstrate the incompatibility between contingency and perfection. What, however, is Hartshorne's criterion of necessity? It is precisely that which we have contended cannot be legitimately affirmed if we take his present view on relations seriously—namely, the coextensiveness of the divine essence with all actuality, which notion, we have seen, is dependent upon the idealistic premise of an omniscient mind in terms of whose contents reality is to be defined. Having rejected the basic epistemological foundation of Hartshorne's thought as being axiomatically irreconcilable with the mutual exclusiveness of contemporary occasions, we therefore conclude that neither his doctrine of the divine essence nor the reformulation of the ontological argument which is systematically dependent on it can be sustained.

Moreover, Hartshorne's doctrine of the divine actuality must be reworked so as to eliminate any tendency to speak of it as all-inclusive without qualification or to identify it *simpliciter* with all actuality as such. That Hartshorne clearly has made this identification may be cited from *The Logic of Perfection* (p. 38) where he says: "...the divine actuality is all actuality," and again, "His actuality...is all-inclusive."

The reason that Hartshorne makes this kind of affirmation is because the idealistic structure of his theism inclines him to conceive of perfection in terms of wholeness or all-inclusiveness.[32] There can be nothing in addition to God, taken as the all-inclusive whole of reality (DR 79, MVG 349). If that were not the case, Hartshorne argues, then God would be only a part of reality, albeit the supreme constituent. But, the religious consciousness would be offended by the impiety of a totality, God-*and*-the-world, which would be greater than God alone.[33]

---

[31] "Metaphysics and the Modality of Existential Judgments," in Ivor Leclerc, ed., *The Relevance of Whitehead* (London: Allen and Unwin, 1961), p. 116; "God's Existence: A Conceptual Problem," in Sidney Hook, ed., *Religious Experience and Truth: A Symposium* (New York: New York University Press, 1961), p. 217.

[32] "The Idea of God—Literal or Analogical?" *The Christian Scholar* 39/2 (June, 1956), 131; *Man's Vision of God*, pp. 201, 293.

[33] *Philosophers Speak of God* (with William L. Reese) (Chicago: The University of Chicago Press, 1953), p. 19.

Now if Hartshorne's conception of the all-inclusiveness of God is amended in favor of a view which allows for an ontological distinction between God and the world, then one does have a totality which is greater than God alone, namely the togetherness of God and whatever else there may be. However, this need not imply in any way the consequent imperfection of deity, for Hartshorne's categories would still enable him to speak of God as "the self-surpassing surpasser of all"—a conception which clearly conveys the notion of perfection without the connotation of all-inclusive, metaphysical wholeness.

CHAPTER VII

IDEAS AND THESES OF PROCESS PHILOSOPHERS

Charles Hartshorne

A. Process Philosophers of the Past

A — Samuel Alexander (1859-1938)
B — Henri Bergson (1859-1941)
Bou — Emile Boutroux (1845-1921)
Bu — Buddhists (ca. 100-)
D — John Dewey (1859-1952)
F — G. T. Fechner (1801-1884)
H — David Hume (1711-1777)
J — William James (1842-1910)
L — Jules Lequier (1814-1862)
M — Karl Marx (1818-1883)
N — Friedrich Nietzsche (1844-1900)
NB — Nicolas Berdyaev (1874-1948)
P — C. S. Peirce (1839-1912)
S — Fausto Socinus (1539-1604)
Sch — F. W. J. von Schelling (1775-1854)
W — A. N. Whitehead (1861-1947)
WPM — Wm. Pepperell Montague (1873-1953)

There is a case for including Hegel in the above list. Indeed, since Kant, and with the exceptions of Bradley, Royce, Russell, Nicolai Hartmann, Santayana, Weiss, and Findlay, metaphysics or speculative philosophy has been almost exclusively process philosophy, taking the term in a broad sense. Yet the critics of metaphysics tend to ignore process philosophers, among whom Croce, Collingwood, and Heidegger should probably be included. Several thinkers in modern India, e.g., Sri Jiva, Mukerji, and Iqbal, could be added. Also Renouvier and Teilhard de Chardin in France; DeWitt H. Parker and E. S. Brightman in the United States; and, with more reservations, Bernardino Varisco in Italy.

B. Common Theses (accepted, or at least not denied, by all or most process thinkers).

1. Becoming includes being; there is a partly new universe each time it is referred to.

2. The future is really open or partly indeterminate (even for God: F, L, NB, S, P, W, WPM).

3. Causal determinism is not absolute; creative freedom (not fully determined, though influenced, by causal conditions) is real: B, Bou, D, F, J, L, N, NB, P, S, W, WPM.

4. "Substance" is defined through "event" or "process", and not vice versa: A, Bu, D, H, J, M, N, W.

5. The laws of nature evolve: B, Bou, P, W.

6. Experience (human or nonhuman) is coextensive with reality (psychical or nonmaterialistic monism, panpsychism or psychicalism). Exceptions: D, M; not decided or clear: J, L, NB.

7. Memory, as givenness of the past, is basic in reality. Especially B, P, W.

8. There are both internal and external relations, both dependence and independence (moderate pluralism). Especially J, P, W.

9. Social relations are pervasive in experience and reality: P ("agapism"), W ("feeling of feeling").

10. Self-interest is *not* the principle of all motivation or the justification of altruism: Bu, H, M, P, W.

11. Some version of the pragmatic theory of meaning is correct: D, J, M, N, P, W.

12. The "ontological principle" (W) that universals, abstractions, are real only in concrete actualities (Aristotle) seems to be affirmed, at least implicitly, in all process philosophies.

13. God is in some aspect in process and is influenced by the creatures: A, F, J, L, NB, P, S, Sch, W, WPM. Nontheists: D, M, N; undecided: H.

14. Aesthetic categories are primary: B, P, W.

15. There are incompossible but genuine values: NB, W.

C. Special Contributions of Peirce (who seems not to have influenced Whitehead).

1. Logico-phenomenological method.

2. Firstness, Secondness, Thirdness.

3. Continuity as order of possibilities. In "Synechism" it is also (wrongly?) taken as order of actualities. These possibilities are viewed, not as an eternal multitude of definite essences (Whitehead's "eternal objects"), but rather as an indeterminate unity out of which more definite qualities emerge or "evolve".

4. Continuity of possible sense qualities (feeling qualities) as a special case of C3. (Hartshorne arrived at this view prior to his study of Peirce, but received precious stimulation from Peirce at this point and many others.)

D. Special Contributions of Whitehead (besides his versions of B1-B15)

1. Epochal theory of becoming (anticipated by Bu and J).

2. Strict ultimacy and universality of creativity or creative synthesis

transcending causal determination by the past in *all* concrete cases of becoming, and applicable even to God. (The nearest approximation in previous systems would be Peirce's Tychism and his doctrine of Firstness.)

3. Perception and memory as alike involving "prehension", the direct grasp of *antecedent* events upon which the perceiving or remembering events asymmetrically depend, thereby denying that perceiving and its data are simultaneous. (The nearest approximation would be Peirce's doctrine of immediate memory as a case of Secondness.)

4. Concept of *concrete* prehensions as "feelings *of* feelings" (cf. B9, B14).

5. Identification of prehension with causality (Whitehead's answer to Hume) and a clear doctrine of both external and internal relations.

6. Clear, technical doctrine of "societies" as the enduring substances, things, and persons of common sense (cf. B4), and of "social order" as *the* order of nature.

7. Overcoming the "bifurcation of nature", as in panpsychism (B6), but with (early twentieth century) physics, physiology, and biology taken into account.

8. Concept of the order of nature as aesthetic.

9. Two natures of God (implicit in all theistic process philosophies).

10. Successive "cosmic epochs," each with its own laws.

E. Special Contributions of Hartshorne

(Although he accepts a form of all the items listed under B, C, and D, in some cases, e.g., B2, B6, B8, B9, B10, B13, B14, Hartshorne seems to have reached his convictions relatively independently of the writers mentioned above. Thus he derived the idea of the open future and the process view of God chiefly from W. E. Hocking, one of his teachers, and the rejection of the self-interest theory of motivation from Royce's discussion of "community" and reflection upon his own experience. Similar remarks could, *a fortiori,* be made about Peirce, Berdyaev, and Whitehead, three very independent thinkers.)

1. Development and defense of the theory of sensations as localized, sense-organ-dependent, feelings (the "affective continuum"). This has affinities with B14, C4, and D4, but in bare outline it was derived from others than those listed above, perhaps even largely fron non-philosophers.

2. A logic of categorial contrasts (absolute, relative; abstract, concrete; object, subject; etc.).

3. A logic of contingency and necessity, with these corollaries: a new perspective on the ontological argument, and a new defense of the possibility of metaphysics.

4. Doctrinal matrices: the method of decision by elimination from exhaustive divisions of the doctrinal possibilities.

5. Theistic proofs (six or seven forms) as applications of these doctrinal matrices (E4); use of creative freedom (D2) and the logic of contingency and necessity (E3) to dissolve the classical problem of evil.

6. Defense of the Peircean (less "platonic": C3) version of the onto-logical principle (B12) as against the Whiteheadian one.

7. Clarification of pragmatism (B11) as applied to noncontingent truths or values, denying that the necessary or eternal (E3) can be bad or ugly.

8. Clarification of issues connected with the process view of God (B13): panentheism; "perfection" as "unsurpassability by another"; principle of dual transcendence.

9. Theory of beauty as a mean between extremes in two dimensions (clarification of B14).

10. Primacy of asymmetrical relations and directional order as furnishing support to B2, B3, B7, B8, B9; C2; D3, D5; E2.

E1 is expounded chiefly in *The Philosophy and Psychology of Sensation*, but is sketched in *Creative Synthesis and Philosophic Method*, chapter 15. For E3, E5, E9, and E10, *Creative Synthesis* is indispensable. E3, E4, E6, and E8 are dealt with in several works, especially *Creative Synthesis, The Logic of Perfection*, and *Anselm's Discovery*. For E7, see *The Logic of Perfection*, chapter 12.

Bibliography

A. Books by Charles Hartshorne and Alfred North Whitehead mentioned in the text, listed alphabetically by their associated symbols:

AD — Hartshorne, *Anselm's Discovery.* LaSalle, Illinois: Open Court, 1965.

AI — Whitehead, *Adventures of Ideas.* New York: Macmillan, 1933.

BH — Hartshorne, *Beyond Humanism: Essays in the New Philosophy of Nature.* Chicago: Willett, Clark & Company, 1937. Bison Book Edition, with new Preface, Lincoln: University of Nebraska Press, 1968.

CN — Whitehead, *The Concept of Nature.* Cambridge: Cambridge University Press, 1920.

CSPM — Hartshorne, *Creative Synthesis and Philosophic Method.* London: SCM Press; LaSalle, Illinois: Open Court, 1970.

DR — Hartshorne, *The Divine Relativity: A Social Conception of God.* New Haven: Yale University Press, 1948.

FR — Whitehead, *The Function of Reason.* Princeton: Princeton University Press, 1929.

LP — Hartshorne, *The Logic of Perfection, and Other Essays in Neoclassical Metaphysics.* LaSalle, Illinois: Open Court, 1962.

MT — Whitehead, *Modes of Thought.* New York: Macmillan, 1938.

MVG — Hartshorne, *Man's Vision of God and the Logic of Theism.* Chicago: Willett, Clark & Company, 1941. Hamden, Conn.: Archon Books, 1964.

NTT — Hartshorne, *A Natural Theology for Our Time.* LaSalle, Illinois: Open Court, 1967.

OD — Hartshorne, "An Outline and Defense of the Argument for the Unity of Being in the Absolute or Divine Good." Ph.D. Thesis, Harvard University May, 1923. OD numbers followed by "d" refer to the seven-page digest while page numbers without the "d" refer to the body of the dissertation.

PPS — Hartshorne, *The Philosophy and Psychology of Sensation.* Chicago: University of Chicago Press, 1934. Port Washington, N. Y.: Kennikat Press, 1968.

PR — Whitehead, *Process and Reality.* New York: Macmillan, 1929.

PSG — Hartshorne, *Philosophers Speak of God* (with William L. Reese). Chicago: University of Chicago Press, 1953.

RM — Whitehead, *Religion in the Making.* New York: Macmillan, 1926.

RSP — Hartshorne, *Reality as Social Process: Studies in Metaphysics and Religion.* Glencoe: Free Press; Boston: Beacon Press, 1953; New York: Hafner, 1971.

SMW — Whitehead, *Science and the Modern World.* New York: Macmillan, 1926.

WP — Hartshorne, *Whitehead's Philosophy: Selected Essays, 1935-1970.* Lincoln: University of Nebraska Press, 1972.

B. Articles by Hartshorne mentioned in the text and/or contained in *Whitehead's Philosophy: Selected Essays, 1935-1970.* In addition to the asterisked items, this book contains an introductory first chapter, "Whitehead after Forty-five Years," pp. 1-8.

* "On Some Criticisms of Whitehead's Philosophy." *The Philosophical Review* 44/4 (July, 1935), 323-44. WP, chapter 3, pp. 21-40.

"Metaphysics for Positivists." *Philosophy of Science* 2/3 (July, 1935), 287-303.

* "The Compound Individual," pp. 193-220 in *Philosophical Essays for Alfred North Whitehead,* ed. Otis H. Lee. New York: Longmans, Green & Co., 1936. WP, chapter 4, pp. 41-62.

Review of Rasvihari Das, *The Philosophy of Whitehead. The Philosophical Review* 48/2 (March, 1939), 23-31.

"The Interpretation of Whitehead (Reply to John W. Blyth)." *The Philosophical Review* 48/4 (July, 1939), 415-23.

* "Whitehead's Idea of God," pp. 513-59 in *The Philosophy of Alfred North Whitehead,* ed. Paul A. Schilpp. Evanston and Chicago: Northwestern University Press, 1941. WP, chapter 5, pp. 63-98.

PB-296-2
5-41
C

104

Review of John Blyth, *Whitehead's Theory of Knowledge*. *Philosophy and Phenomenological Research* 3/3 (March, 1943), 372-75.

* "Is Whitehead's God the God of Religion?" *Ethics* 53/3 (April, 1943), 219-27. WP, chapter 6, pp. 99-110.

"Ideal Knowledge Defines Reality: What Was True in 'Idealism'." *The Journal of Philosophy* 43/21 (October 10, 1946), 573-82.

"Letter." *The Journal of Philosophy* 43 (December 19, 1946), 724.

"The Rationalistic Criterion in Metaphysics." *Philosophy and Phenomenological Research* 8/3 (March, 1948), 436-47.

* "Whitehead's Metaphysics," pp. 25-41 in *Whitehead and the Modern World*, by Victor Lowe, Charles Hartshorne, and A. H. Johnson. Boston: Beacon Press, 1950. WP, chapter 2, pp. 9-20.

"Panpsychism," pp. 323-44 in *A History of Philosophical Systems*, ed. Vergilius Ferm. New York: The Philosophical Library, 1950.

"The Divine Relativity and Absoluteness: A Reply." *The Review of Metaphysics* 4/1 (September, 1950), 31-60.

"Tillich's Doctrine of God," in *The Theology of Paul Tillich*, eds. C. W. Kegley and R. W. Bretall. New York: Macmillan, 1952.

"The Monistic Theory of Expression." *The Journal of Philosophy* 50 (July 2, 1953), 425-34.

* "Whitehead's Philosophy of Reality as Socially-Structured Process." *Chicago Review* 8/2 (Spring-Summer, 1954), 60-77. WP, chapter 7, pp. 111-24.

"Causal Necessities: An Alternative to Hume." *The Philosophical Review* 63/4 (October, 1954), 479-99.

"Some Empty Though Important Truths." *The Review of Metaphysics* 8/4 (June, 1955), 553-68. LP, chapter 12, pp. 280-97.

"Royce's Mistake—and Achievement." *The Journal of Philosophy* 53/3 (February 2, 1956), 123-30.

* "Whitehead and Berdyaev: Is There Tragedy in God?" *The Journal of Religion* 37/2 (April, 1957), 71-84. WP, chapter 13, pp. 183-208.

"Whitehead on Process: A Reply to Professor Eslick." *Philosophy and Phenomenological Research* 18/4 (June, 1958), 514-20.

"Metaphysical Statements as Non-Restrictive and Existential." *The Review of Metaphysics* 12/1 (September, 1958), 35-47.

"The Logical Structure of Givenness." *The Philosophical Quarterly* 8 (October, 1958), 307-16.

"The Philosophy of Creative Synthesis." *The Journal of Philosophy* 55/22 (October 23, 1958), 944-53.

* "Whitehead and Contemporary Philosophy," pp. 21-43 in *The Relevance of Whitehead*, ed. Ivor Leclerc. London: Allen and Unwin, 1961. WP, chapter 10, pp. 141-60.

"Metaphysics and the Modality of Existential Judgments," pp. 107-21 in *The Relevance of Whitehead*, ed. Ivor Leclerc. London: Allen and Unwin, 1961.

"Hume's Metaphysics and Its Present-Day Influence." *The New Scholasticism* 35/2 (April, 1961), 152-71.

"The Social Structure of Experience." *Philosophy* 36/137 (April and July, 1961), 97-111.

"The Structure of Givenness." *The Philosophical Forum* 18 (1960-61), 22-39.

"God's Existence: A Conceptual Problem," pp. 211-19 in *Religious Experience and Truth: A Symposium*, ed. Sidney Hook. New York: New York University Press, 1961.

"Tillich and the Other Great Tradition." *Anglican Theological Review* 43 (July, 1961), 245-59.

"Absolute Objects and Relative Subjects: A Reply." *The Review of Metaphysics* 15/1 (September, 1961), 174-88.

* "Whitehead, The Anglo-American Philosopher-Scientist." *Proceedings of the American Catholic Philosophical Association*, vol. 35, pp. 163-71. 1961. WP, chapter 9, pp. 129-40, under new title: "Whitehead's Generalizing Power."

* "Whitehead's Theory of Prehension," pp. 167-68 in *Actas: Segundo Congreso Extraordinario Interamericano de Filosofía*, 22-26 July 1961. San José, Costa Rica: Imprenta Nacional, 1962. WP, chapter 8, pp. 125-27.

"Present Prospects for Metaphysics." *The Monist* 47/2 (Winter, 1963), 188-210.

"Further Fascination of the Ontological Argument: Replies to Richardson." *Union Seminary Quarterly Review* 18/3, part I (March, 1963), 244-45.

* "Whitehead's Novel Intuition," pp. 18-26 in *Alfred North Whitehead: Essays on His Philosophy*, ed. George L. Kline. Englewood Cliffs: Prentice-Hall, 1963. WP, chapter 11, pp. 161-70.

"From Colonial Beginnings to Philosophical Greatness." *The Monist* 48/3 (July, 1964), 317-31.

"Interrogation of Charles Hartshorne," pp. 321-54 in *Philosophical Interrogations*, eds. Sydney and Beatrice Rome. New York: Holt, Rinehart and Winston, 1964.

"Idealism and Our Experience of Nature," pp. 70-80 in *Philosophy, Religion and the Coming World Civilization*, ed. Leroy S. Rouner. The Hague: Martinus Nijhoff, 1966.

"Royce and the Collapse of Idealism." *Revue Internationale de Philosophie* 21 (1967), 46-59.

"The Case for Idealism." *The Philosophical Forum* 1 (n.s. Fall, 1968), 7-23.

* "Whitehead and Ordinary Language." *The Southern Journal of Philosophy* 7/4 (Winter, 1969-70), 437-45. WP, chapter 12, pp. 171-82.

"Whitehead in French Perspective: A Review Article." *The Thomist* 33/3 (July, 1969), 573-81. A review of Alix Parmentier, *La Philosophie de Whitehead et le Problème de Dieu* (Paris: Beauchesne, 1968).

"The Development of My Philosophy," pp. 211-28 in *Contemporary American Philosophy, Second Series*, ed. John E. Smith. London: Allen and Unwin; New York: Humanities Press, 1970.